HEINEMANN
GEOGRAPHY

Series editor: John Hopkin

People &
THE EUROPEAN
COMMUNITY

FRED MARTIN AUBREY WHITTLE

LONDON BOROUGH OF HAVERING

SACRED HEART OF MARY
GIRLS SCHOOL
UPMINSTER

HEINEMANN
EDUCATIONAL

GW01388367

Heinemann Educational
a division of Heinemann Educational Books Ltd.
Halley Court, Jordan Hill, Oxford OX2 8EJ

OXFORD   LONDON   EDINBURGH
MADRID   ATHENS   BOLOGNA   PARIS
MELBOURNE   SYDNEY   AUCKLAND   SINGAPORE
TOKYO   IBADAN   NAIROBI   HARARE
GABORONE   PORTSMOUTH NH (USA)

© Fred Martin and Aubrey Whittle 1991

First published 1991

**A catalogue record for this book is available from
the British Library**

ISBN 0 453 35194 X

Designed and produced by Gecko Limited, Bicester, Oxon

Printed and bound in Spain by Mateu Cromo

Note to teachers
Details of National Curriculum Statements of Attainment covered are
given on the pupil spreads; italics indicate partial coverage. A summary
of the Statements of Attainment and Programme of Study coverage is
given in the matrix and teacher's notes in the accompanying Teacher's
Resource Pack.

Acknowledgements

Thanks are due to the following for permission to reproduce copyright
material: Agency for Corporate Development, Ile de France, p. 25(F, H);
Birmingham Technology Ltd, p. 17(C); Bryan, Constantinidi and
Brightwell Ltd, p. 29(H); George Philip Ltd, p. 7(G); Professor Russell
King/Butterworth-Heinemann, p. 39(F); Publicity Office, Association Loi
de 1901, p. 32(C); Regional Council of Brittany, p. 32(B); Touring Club
Italiano, p. 45(C, D and E); Triplex Lloyd Plc, p. 19(C);

The Publishers would also like to thank the following for permission to
reproduce photographs: J. Allister/Grange School, p. 9(F, H); Aspect
Picture Library, pp. 4(D), 27(F), 44(B); Birmingham Technology Ltd, p.
17(C,D); British Nuclear Fuels, p. 10(D); Brittany Ferries, p. 29(H);
Brittany Prince/BCB Ltd, p. 31(F); J. Allan Cash Ltd, pp. 4(A, B), 6(B, C,
D), 8(A), 20(B, C), 21(F), 23(D), 25(E), 27(D, E), 28(B); Rick Cope, 13(H);
Veronique Dolo, p. 32(D); Earth Satellite Corporation, p. 46(A); Greg
Evans Photo Library, p. 47(E); John Hopkin, p. 43(F); Hutchison Picture
Library, pp. 23(E), 47(F); Impact Photos, p. 21(E); John Killingbeck, pp.
38(A, B, D), 40(A, B, C); Russell King, pp. 39(F), 41(D); Kirkstone Green
Slate Quarries Ltd, p. 10(B); Lake District National Park, p. 13(E); A.
Maier, p. 24(A); Fred Martin, pp. 8(B, D), 9 (G, I), 11 (G, H, I, J), 12(B, C,
D), 13(I), 28(C), 29(F, G, I), 30(A, B, C), 31(H); Meteo France, p. 32(C);
Peugeot Talbot Motor Co., p. 16(B); Regional Council of Brittany, p.
32(B); Saras SpA, p. 42(D); Science Photo Library, p. 22(B); Siege
Social, p. 33(E); Triplex Lloyd/Jefferson Air Photography, pp. 18(A),
19(D); Penny Tweedie/ Impact Photos, p. 6(A); Colin Underhill/
Barnaby's Picture Library, p. 14(B); VSEL, p. 10(C);

Cover photograph by J. Allan Cash Ltd

The Publishers have made every effort to trace copyright holders.
However, if any material has been incorrectly acknowledged, we would
be pleased to correct this at the earliest opportunity.

Contents

Introduction
Into Europe   4
The UK
Contrasts in the UK   6
Lake District landscapes   8
Lakeland work   10
Country matters   12
The growth of towns and industries   14
Locations for industry   16
Park Lane in change   18
France
Living in France   20
The Ile de France region   22
Working Paris   24
Plans for the region   26
The Brittany coast   28
Brittany farmers   30
Hi-tech Brittany   32
Italy
Seeing Italy   34
Patterns and people   36
The rural heart of the south   38
Change in Aliano   40
Support for the south   42
The 'golden triangle'   44
Patterns of land use   46
Glossary   48

Into Europe

▲ **A** *A fjord inlet on Norway's coast*

▲ **B** *A rural landscape with vineyards in Andalusia, south-west Spain*

Any trail across Europe takes you through a constantly changing landscape (photos A and B). Each area has its own climate, rocks, relief, soils, and vegetation. These natural features combine to give special landscapes (C). A large area with a similar kind of landscape is called a **geographic region**.

1 Draw a chart for the two photos A and B using these headings:
   - Location (where they are)
   - Relief (shape of the land)
   - Vegetation (plants)
   - Climate
   - Rocks and soils

   Fill in the chart with notes to describe what you see.

2 Study diagram C.
   Use photos A and B to describe some ways in which some of the natural features are linked. (Example: how rocks are linked to soils).

3 Work in pairs. Each choose either photo A or B.
   a List the ways in which land is being used.
   b In what ways do you think that natural features have affected how the land is used?
   c Draw a sketch of the photo you have chosen, to show how the land could be used in different ways.
   d Explain why you think your ideas for the use of the land might be suitable.

4 Using an atlas, work in a group to draw a trail, either from north to south or east to west, on a large outline map of Europe.
   At every 5° latitude or longitude, add notes and sketches to show the natural features for the area such as:
   - relief and rivers
   - natural vegetation
   - climate.

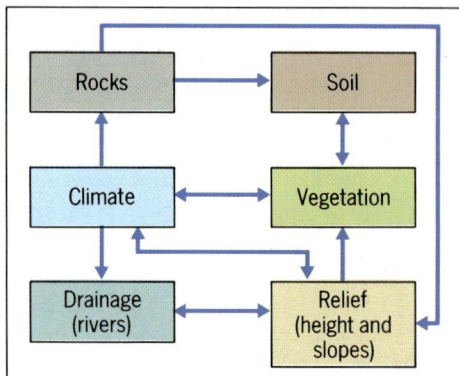

C *Links between natural features*

People choose how to use the land and make a living in different ways. Natural features affect this choice. In mountain areas with harsh climates, choices may be limited. In lowland areas with milder climates, the choice is much wider.

5 Describe some ways in which people in European countries have come closer together. Use headlines D and the text below them to help you. Think about:
- places visited on holiday
- foods
- words people use
- goods people buy.

Visitor figures up again

Berlin Wall falls. East and West Germany unite.

Satellites bring European TV to your home

Channel Tunnel linked at last!

European government ministers agree pollution plan

Eurovision song time again

In the past, people in European countries fought wars against each other. Today they travel as tourists, workers and to visit friends (D). Goods are bought and sold between them. Even the division between east and west European countries is being broken down.

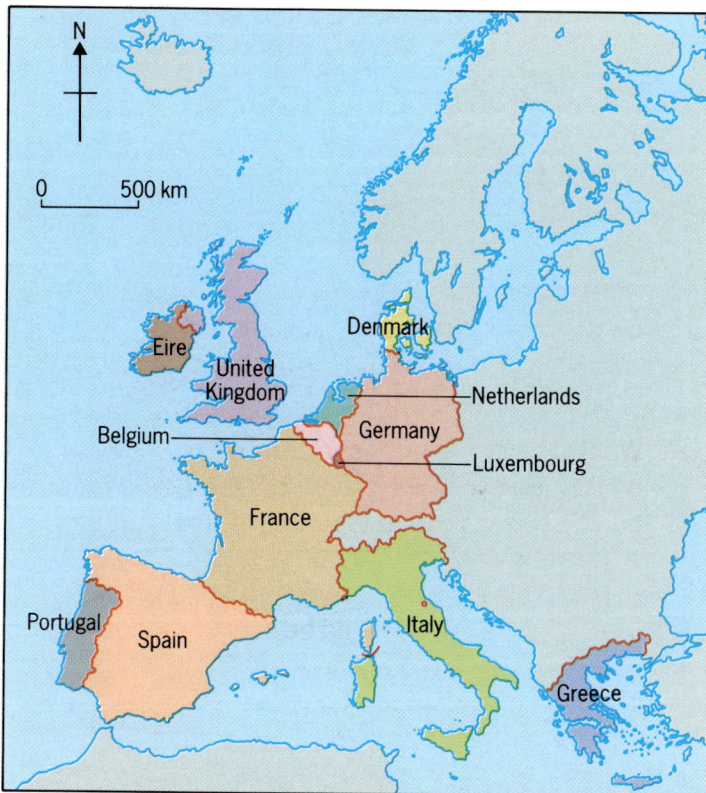

E *The European Community countries*

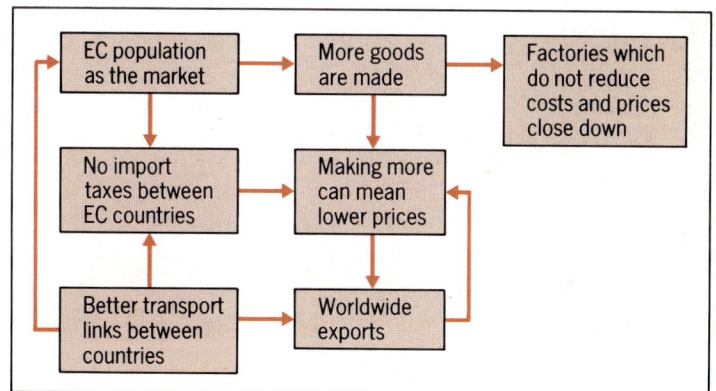

▲ **F** *How the EC helps trade*

The **European Community (EC)** is a group of 12 European countries (E). More may join in the future. The EC countries want to make it easier to buy and sell goods between them. The buying and selling of goods is called **trading**. With more trading between more people, goods can be made and sold more cheaply (F). This should help give people a better standard of living.

6 Use map E to make a list of the countries which are members of the EC.

7 a Using diagram F, explain what is meant by trading.
 b How can making it easier to trade keep down the costs of goods?

c How might some people lose out on easier trading?
d How can easier trade help give people a better standard of living?

Contrasts in the UK

A *Sheffield*

B *The Fens*

C *The Scottish Highlands*

D *South Wales*

Thinly peopled, mountainous, mostly moorland and poor quality grazing.

Routes mostly run north-south, few connections east-west. Settlements linear in shape and confined to valleys. Evidence of factories and mines.

Route network not well developed, flat relief, a rich agricultural area of scattered towns and villages.

Highly urbanized, dense network of roads, large population.

▲ **E** *Captions describing areas A–D*

SIMPLE sketch of the photo. Draw the box to match the photo shape.

SIMPLE sketch of the route pattern and some settlement.

The location of this landscape is the UK. Use names such as South West England.

Description of the photo and route map using the caption E as a guide.

▲ **F** *Area information chart*

With its 57 million people, the UK is the third most populated country in the EC. Although it is small in area, it has a variety of landscapes.

6

1 Photos A to D show four contrasting landscapes in the UK. Pair up each photo with one of the captions E and a map from G.

2 Complete a copy of chart F for each landscape. Use an atlas to work out where each locality is.

▽ G Road maps

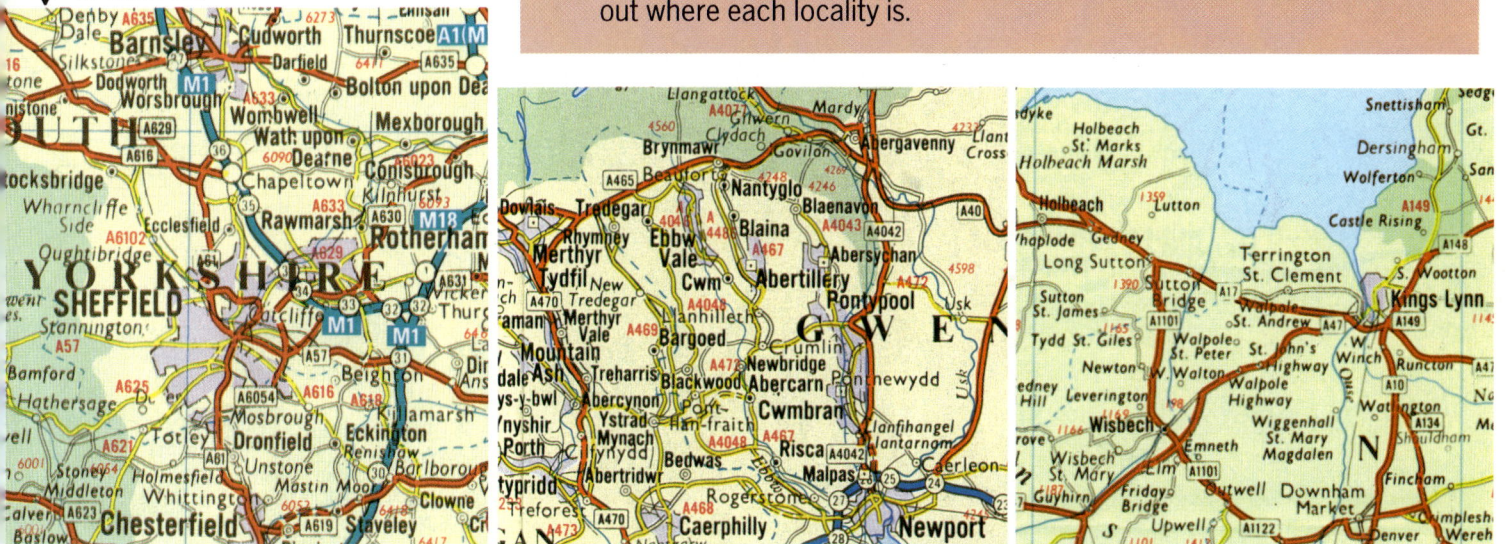

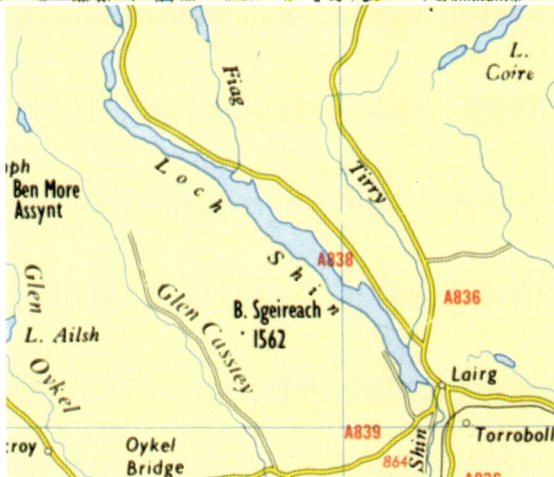

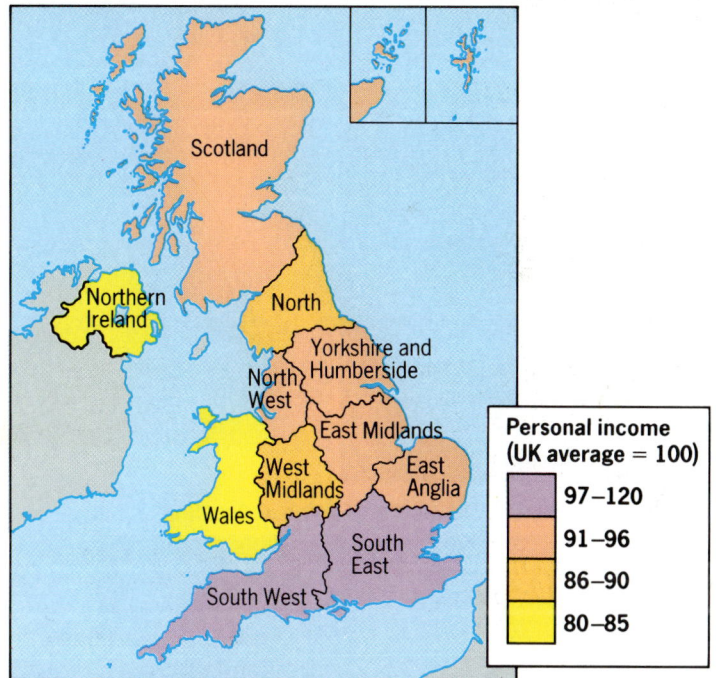

By world standards the UK is a wealthy country. The population receive high levels of health care and education. They earn enough money to buy cars, hi-fi equipment and annual holidays. Wealth, health, leisure, education and housing can be used to measure a person's **quality of life**. Map H shows a pattern of wealth in the UK.

Personal income (UK average = 100)
- 97–120
- 91–96
- 86–90
- 80–85

△ H Regions of the UK

3 a What is 'personal income'?
   b Why could this be a useful way of showing the 'quality' of a person's life?
   c Describe the pattern shown by map H. Mention the wealthiest and least wealthy areas.
   d Make a list of five other ways you could measure and map the quality of life in the UK (e.g. pollution).

4 a Describe any differences in the quality of life of various people in your home area.
   b The people of Scotland have below average incomes. Photo C shows a part of Scotland. In what way might the Scottish people living there have a better quality of life than people in a more prosperous part of the UK?

Lake District landscapes

▼ **A** *A glacial valley with Lake Buttermere*

The Lake District has a special kind of landscape (A and B). Natural processes and a long history of settlement have given it the natural and land use features that make it so distinctive (C–H).

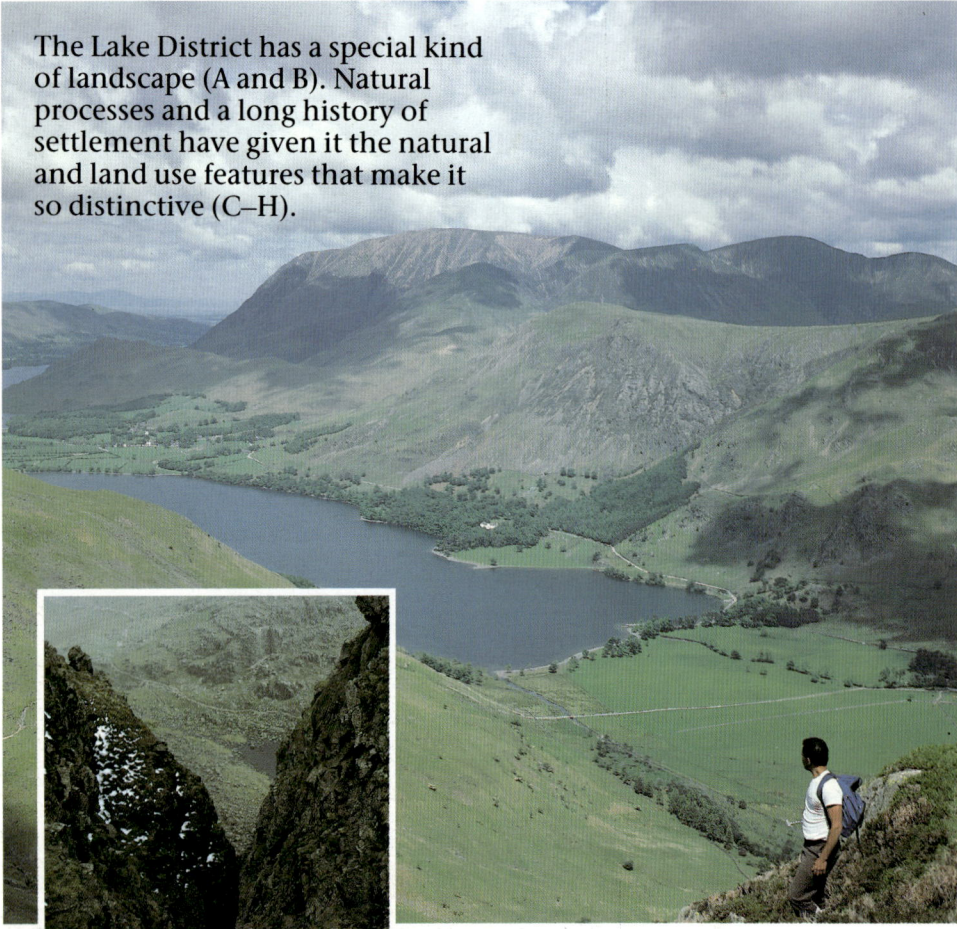

▲**B** *Weathered rock on the Old Man of Coniston*

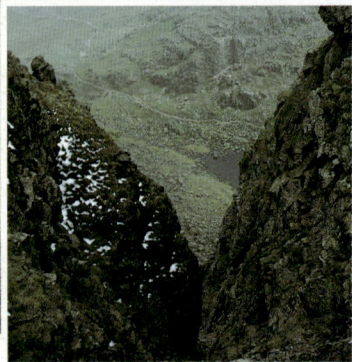

The Lake District

Physical background

- Rocks are mainly ancient limestones, slates and from volcanoes.
- The long **ribbon lakes** and deep, wide valleys were shaped by glaciers.
- Ice sheets have rounded the upper slopes and mountain tops.
- Ice has scooped out hollows in the mountains; some are now lakes called **tarns**.
- Steep ridges called **arêtes** formed as ice cut back into the mountain peaks.
- Ice expands and shatters rocks; these fall as **screes** on the valley sides.
- Waterfalls happen when streams fall into deep glacial valleys.
- Mountain streams cut steep-sided valleys.

▲**C** *Landscape features of the Lake District*

D *Bluebells in a deciduous wood*

1 Use an atlas map of the Lake District to answer a-d.
   a Which county is the Lake District in?
   b Name the highest mountain peak in the area.
   c Name the mountain range.
   d Name three long valley-bottom lakes.

2 Study photos A and B and notes C.
   a Describe two ways in which lakes have been formed.
   b How do streams shape the landscape?
   c How does ice break up the rock?
   d How has ice changed the shape of the mountains?

3 Does the scene in photo D seem to be natural? Explain your answer.

Lake District land use

- Some lakes are used as **reservoirs** for water supply.
- Sheep graze on the mountain sides.
- The Forestry Commission plants trees on upland areas and on valley slopes.
- Valley bottoms are used for cattle rearing.
- There are signs of mining, past and present.
- About 10 million day visitors come to the Lake District each year.

E *Land use notes*

F *Land use in the Grisedale Valley*

G *Limestone mining*

H *The Forestry Commission at work*

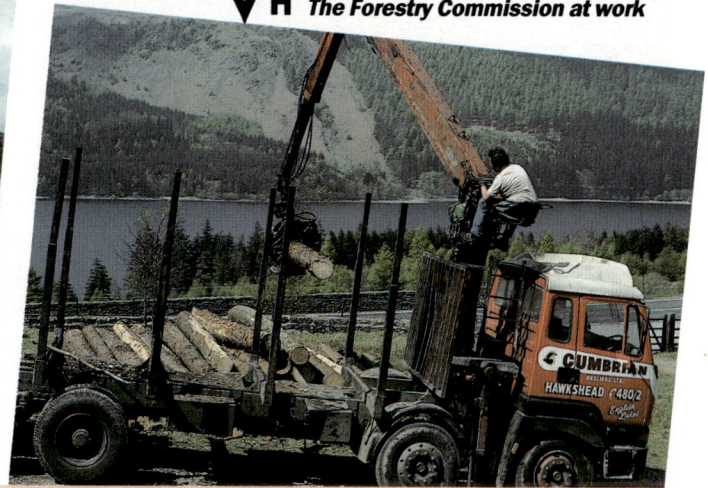

I *Pleasure boats by Lake Windermere*

4 Study notes E and photos F–I.
   a Describe the type of landscape used for rearing sheep.
   b How is farm land used in the valley bottoms?
   c What type of land are trees usually planted on?
   d Why do you think that some rocks in the area might be suitable for quarrying?
   e Why do you think the Lake District is so popular for tourism? Use the photos and information on these pages to give your reasons.

Lakeland work

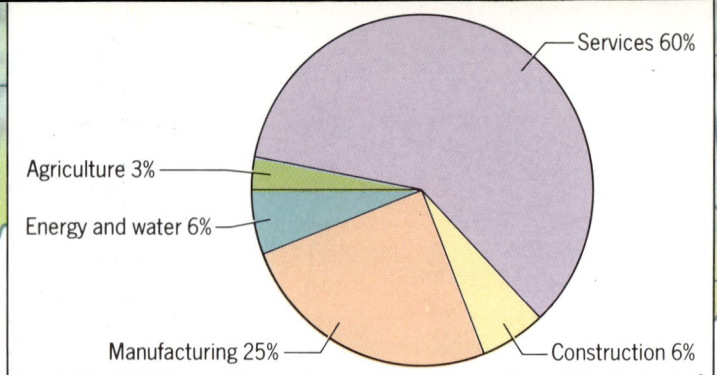

A *Employment in Cumbria*

- Services 60%
- Agriculture 3%
- Energy and water 6%
- Manufacturing 25%
- Construction 6%

People in the Lake District valleys mainly live in small towns and villages where there is little choice of work. The types of work people do in an area is called the **employment structure** (A). Some jobs, such as quarrying, are in the valleys where the rock is found (B). Workers also travel daily to a small number of larger firms on the coast (C and D).

1   Study an atlas map of Cumbria.
   a Draw a sketch map to show the location of these main towns:
   - Carlisle ● Whitehaven ● Barrow-in-Furness
   - Workington ● Kendal
   b What does your atlas tell you about the number of people in these settlements? Study the atlas key, and give figures in your answer.

Name: *Kirkstone Green Slate Quarries Ltd*
Locations: *Kirkstone Pass and Skelwith Bridge (near Ambleside)*
Products: *quarrying slates*
Workforce: *60*

B *Mining in Kirkstone, Cumbria*

Name: *Vickers Engineering*
Location: *Barrow-in-Furness*
Products: *submarines and marine engineering*
Workforce: *7500*

C *Building submarines at Barrow-in-Furness*

D *Nuclear power plant at Sellafield*

Name: *British Nuclear Fuels Limited*
Location: *Sellafield*
Products: *nuclear power*
Workforce: *10 000*

2   Read the employment structure figures in A.
   a Now rule a 10 × 10 grid of 100 squares. Each square represents 1%.
   Using different colours, shade in the right number of squares for each type of work.
   Add a key.
   Give your diagram a title.
   b What do you notice about the figures for Cumbria?

3   Study the information in B, C and D.
   a Choose one of the three firms.
   Draw a diagram to show what might happen if the firm either closed down or cut back its workforce. Include details of:
   - other firms that supply it with parts
   - service firms such as transport and banking
   - shops and services workers use
   - unemployment and migration to other parts of the country.
   b Why do you think jobs in these firms are so important to people in the Lake District valleys?

4 Study the figures in E.
  a Give some examples of jobs in service industries.
  b Explain why you think jobs were lost in primary and secondary industries, but the number of service jobs increased.

5 Study the figures in F, and photos G, H, I and J.
  a How does tourism bring jobs to Cumbria? Give examples.
  b Explain how tourism can bring work and money to farmers.

6 Draw up an advert for any job involved in looking after the tourists in the Lake District. Remember to include:
  ● the type of work
  ● the working hours
  ● what experience is needed
  ● whether the job is permanent or temporary
  ● the wages
  ● other details.

7 Would you like to work in the tourist industry in the Lake District? Explain your answer, giving advantages and disadvantages.

Primary (farming, mining, forestry)	−229
Secondary and construction (manufacturing and building)	−5 857
Services	+7 573

E *Gains and losses in employment in Cumbria, 1981–84*

Number of jobs for every £100 000 spent by tourists	
Accommodation of all kinds	61
Caravans and camping	8
Restaurants and pubs	12
Shops	3
Visitor attractions	13
In Cumbria, there are 25 000 workers employed in tourism.	

F *Employment in tourism*

▽**G** *Tourist shops at Ambleside, Lake Windermere*

▽**I** *and* **J** *A time-share village near Lake Windermere*

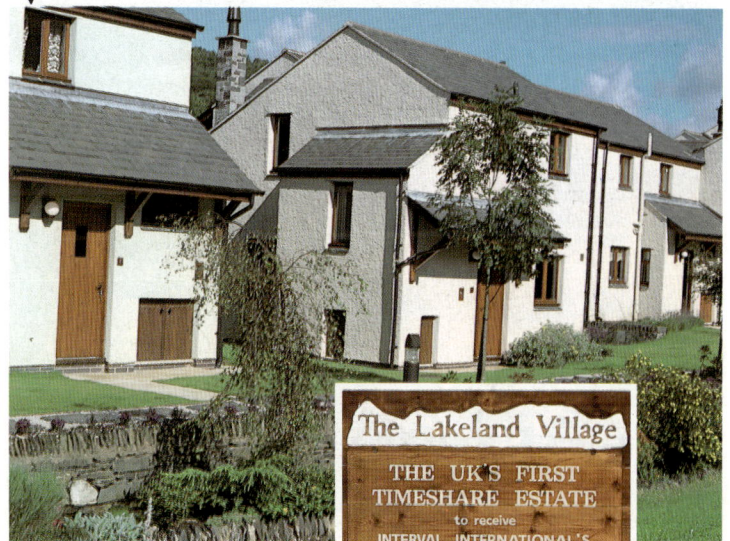

H *Guest house accommodation at Ambleside*

Country matters

There are many advantages to living in the Lake District, with its beautiful landscape; but conserving both the local way of life and the landscape are increasing problems. Tourists are a main cause of these problems (A – D).

LAST BUS HOME
Lack of passengers has forced the bus service to close.

VILLAGE HOMELESS
Young people cannot afford local homes. Too many have been bought as holiday homes by outsiders.

VILLAGE SCHOOL SHOCK
Local authority says it has too few pupils and it is too dear to keep open.

STAMPED OUT
The village post office and store is soon to close. At the moment, only visitor trade is keeping it open.

SURGERY TO SHUT
The village will no longer have its own local doctor. A new group practice will be opened in a nearby town to serve the whole area.

▲A *Newspaper cuttings*

▲B *A traditional cottage in Coniston – properties like this are often bought by outsiders as holiday homes*

▲C *A crowded car park at Ambleside: tourism brings traffic jams to local roads*

D *A new marina and time-share houses on the shores of Lake Windermere*

1 Read the headlines in A.
   a List, in order, what services you think would be most needed to keep people living in a village. Start with the most important.
   b Give some reasons why these village shops and services may have to close.

2 Study the photos B–D.
   a Draw a large sketch to show different ways in which life in a Lake District valley can be changed by tourism.
   b What change do you think would cause the greatest conflict between visitors and local people?

The Lake District is one of the UK's 10 **National Parks** (E and F). It is managed by the Lake District Special Planning Board. On this Board, the National Parks Authority works with planning departments, other conservation groups and local people (G). They aim to make sure that the environment can be enjoyed by both residents and visitors (H and I).

E *The Lake District National Park logo*

LAKE DISTRICT NATIONAL PARK

Some planning rules in the National Park

- Different water activities must be put on different lakes.
- Buildings must be repaired using local building materials in a local style.
- Changes to farms which affect the landscape must be agreed by the Planning Board.
- New building is only allowed for very special reasons.
- Public footpaths must be signposted and kept open.

▲**G** *Some planning rules within the National Park*

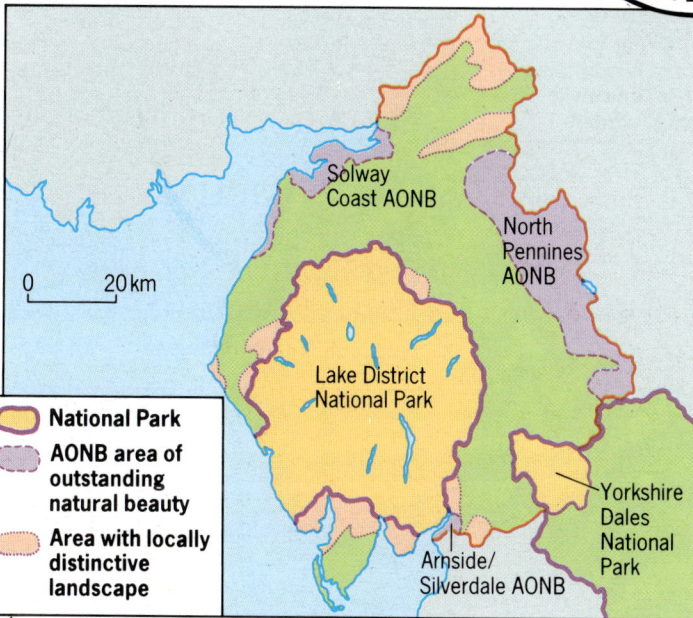

Solway Coast AONB

North Pennines AONB

Lake District National Park

0 — 20 km

🔲 National Park
🔲 AONB area of outstanding natural beauty
🔲 Area with locally distinctive landscape

Arnside/ Silverdale AONB

Yorkshire Dales National Park

▲**F** *Conserved landscapes in Cumbria*

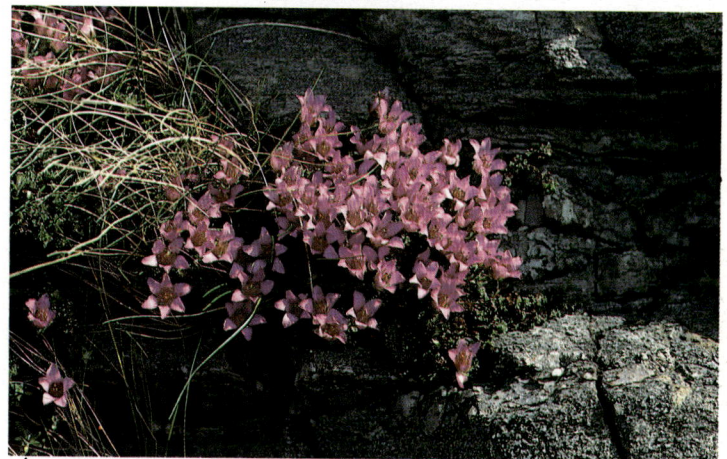

▲**H** *A purple saxifrage: a rare plant under threat from visitors and grazing sheep*

3 a Look again at the text on this page. Which authority manages the Lake District?
  b Draw their symbol, E. Why do you think this symbol was chosen?

4 Using map F decide about how much of Cumbria is taken up by land with some kind of local or national scenic value?

5 Study photos H and I and read the captions. What landscape problems do they show?

6 Read these two statements.
  ● The Lake District should be planned mainly to suit the needs of visitors.
  ● The needs of people who live and work in the Lake District should be given first priority.
  Which of these statements would you most agree with?
  Give reasons for your answers.

I *Mountain footpaths are widened by overuse and scar the slopes*

The growth of towns and industries

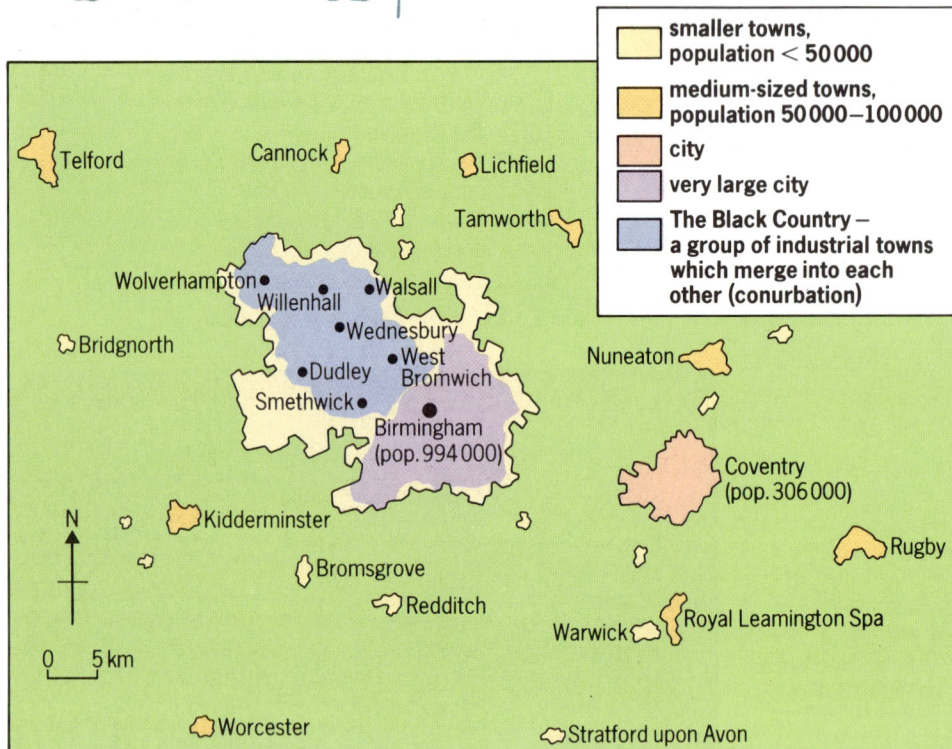

West Midlands conurbation

A *The West Midlands region*

smaller towns,
population < 50 000

medium-sized towns,
population 50 000–100 000

city

very large city

The Black Country –
a group of industrial towns
which merge into each
other (conurbation)

The West Midlands are dominated by a huge built-up area. This urban area is made up of towns which, over the years, have expanded and merged together to become a **conurbation**. The West Midlands conurbation covers an area of 700 square kilometres and has a population of 2.5 million people. The conurbation and the surrounding towns and countryside make up the West Midlands region. A **network** of roads and railway lines connects the conurbation to nearby towns and other parts of the country (B and C).

B *Fast, efficient road routes*

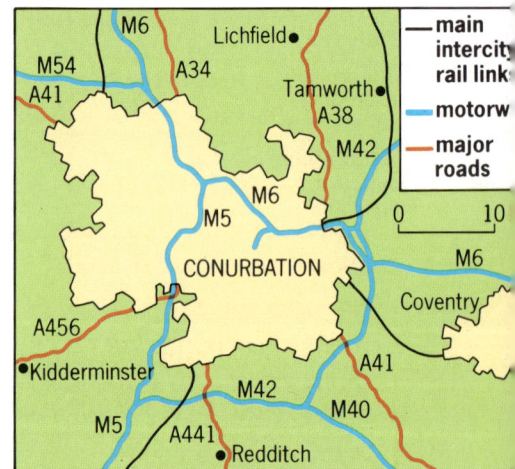

C *The major road and rail network*

1 Study map A and the text on this page.
Write a paragraph describing the West Midlands conurbation. Mention:
   - the cities which make up the conurbation
   - the Black Country and its towns
   - the east-west width, in kilometres
   - the total population
   - the total area.

2 Study photo B and map C.
a Explain why motorways are fast routes.
b Name two motorways which photo B could be.

3 Work in pairs and use an atlas.
a Find the name of a city which is linked to the West Midlands by each of the following:

   ● M6 ● M1 (north) ● M1 (south) ● M5

b Imagine you work for a road haulage company. You deliver to all parts of the UK.
Write a joint report to the managing director of your company recommending that she sets up a base in the West Midlands.

◀ **D** *Reasons for the growth of industry*

▼ **E** *Notes on the West Midlands*

Skills   By 1650 people had the skills to make nails, locks, bits for horses, leather harnesses and cutlery. Iron-making was a long-established industry.

Raw materials   Local resources of coal, iron ore and limestone were used as early as the 14th century. They provided the raw materials for iron to make a variety of metal products.

Ideas and innovators   The Midlands have always had people who were prepared to try out new ideas. These inventions and innovations gave the Midlands industry a head start; for example Murdoch's gas lighting meant factories could work 24 hours a day.

Products   Products such as nuts, nails and springs are small but are high in value for their size. Firms could sell them at a good profit even if they had to be transported long distances to markets such as London or abroad.

Communications   The West Midlands region has benefited from having good communications. It has, in turn, been the centre of the country's canal, rail and road networks.

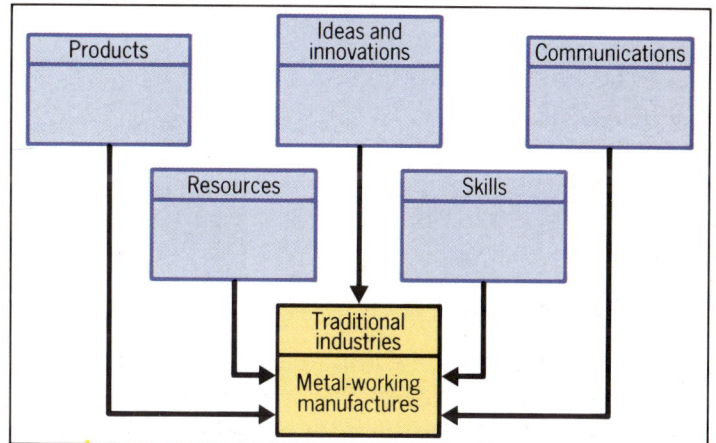

F   *The growth of industry*

In the 200 years between 1650 and 1850, Birmingham and the Black Country were totally changed. What had been a region of countryside and small towns became a landscape of mines, blast furnaces, smoky workshops and metal-product factories.

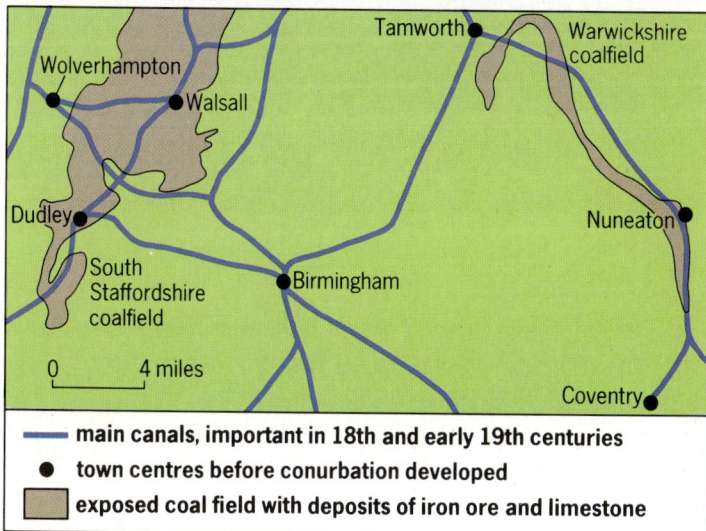

4   Study sketches D and notes E.
   a Match up each sketch with the correct note.
   b Make a large copy of flow diagram F.
   c In each box, draw the correct sketch from D and write a few sentences to summarize the information you have read in E.

5   What features in the West Midlands helped industry to grow? Map G will help you.

main canals, important in 18th and early 19th centuries

town centres before conurbation developed

exposed coal field with deposits of iron ore and limestone

G   *The West Midlands in the 18th century*

Locations for industry

In the West Midlands 30–40% of workers have jobs in the **manufacturing industries**. This is above average for the UK. The West Midlands is a major centre for industry. The big employers in Coventry illustrate this. The reasons why a business or industry sets up at a particular place are called **locational factors**. The choice of Ryton in Coventry for the Peugeot Talbot car assembly plant (B) illustrates these factors.

- There are 50 companies involved in car assembly or component manufacture in Coventry.
- 26 000 people are employed. This is half of all the workers in Coventry's manufacturing jobs.
- The largest employers are car firms: Jaguar has 9 000 workers, Peugeot Talbot has 4 000.

▲ **A** *The car industry in Coventry*

- In Coventry there is a skilled, knowledgeable workforce. Car manufacture is a long-established industry there.
- There are excellent transport facilities. The A45 led to the A1 trunk road which, in turn, took cars to the North, or south to London.
- There is plenty of space to build and expand.
- During World War 2 Ryton was built as a 'shadow' factory in case other vehicle plants in Coventry were bombed.
- Coventry and surrounding towns had car component manufacturers.

B *Aerial photo of the Ryton car plant, and notes explaining its location*

1 What do notes A tell you about the importance of the car industry in Coventry?
2 Study photo B and the notes.
   a Place a sketch of B in the centre of your page.
   b In the space around the sketch, add in the notes from B. Draw an arrow from each note to the correct place on your sketch.

There has been a car industry in Coventry for many years. Newer industries need a different blend of location factors. **Science parks, business parks, industrial parks** and **industrial estates** have some things in common:

- Several workplaces are grouped on their own estate.
- They are served by their own roads and, on some estates, by shops and banks.
- The area was planned out as a whole.
- The firms are compatible (a noisy factory would not go well with an office block).
- The land around is landscaped.
- Adequate car parking is provided.

The location and layout of Aston Science Park (C and D) has some similarities and some differences to the Ryton plant.

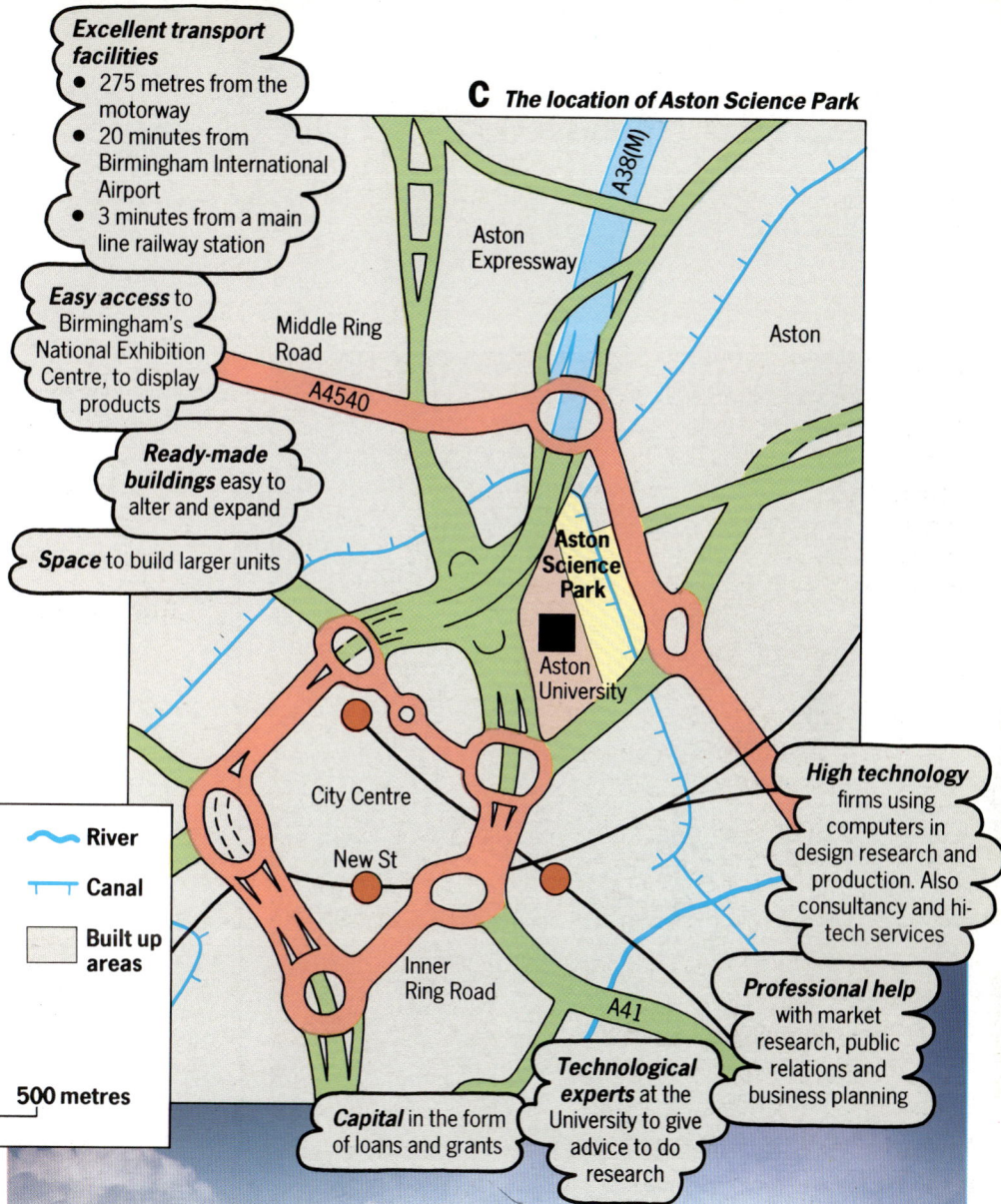

C *The location of Aston Science Park*

Excellent transport facilities
- 275 metres from the motorway
- 20 minutes from Birmingham International Airport
- 3 minutes from a main line railway station

Easy access to Birmingham's National Exhibition Centre, to display products

Ready-made buildings easy to alter and expand

Space to build larger units

High technology firms using computers in design research and production. Also consultancy and hi-tech services

Professional help with market research, public relations and business planning

Technological experts at the University to give advice to do research

Capital in the form of loans and grants

Aston Expressway

Aston

Middle Ring Road

A4540

Aston Science Park

Aston University

City Centre

New St

Inner Ring Road

A41

A38(M)

Legend			
Motorway		River	
Major road		Canal	
Other road		Built up areas	
Railway			
Station			

0 — 500 metres

3 Use map C, photo D and the text on this page to design a poster advertizing the attractions of the Aston Science Park for a business.

4 **a** Compare Aston Science Park in C and D with the Ryton plant in B. Mention:
- the number of businesses
- their location
- landscaping
- ease of access (how easy they are to reach).

b What do you think is the most likely reason for a hi-tech firm to locate at Aston?

D *Aston Science Park*

Park Lane in change

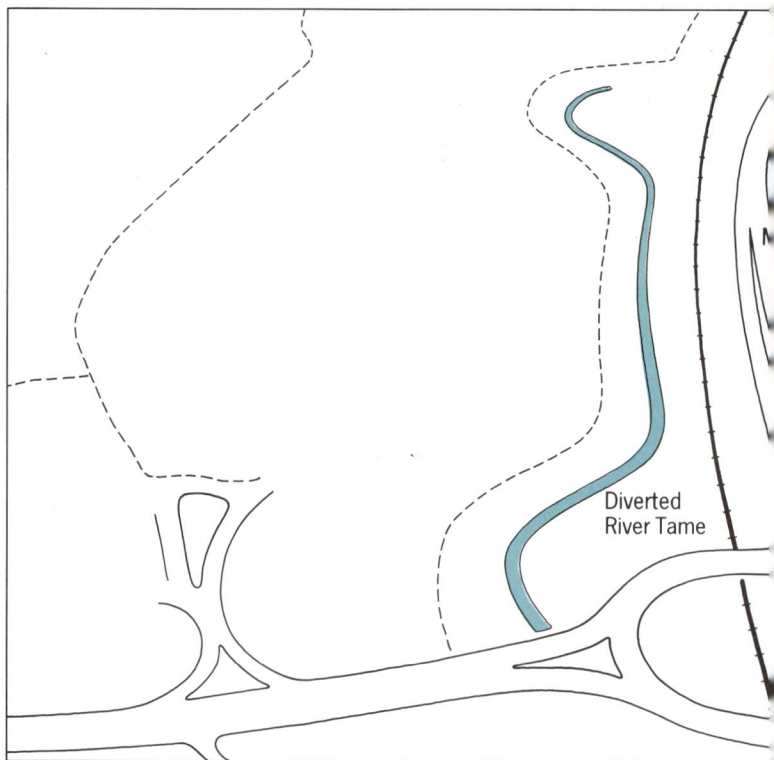

A *Aerial photo of the Park Lane site*

The way land is used in cities is always changing. Factories close and their buildings become derelict. Other land may lay waste or be used for tipping. Such **derelict land** is unsightly and wasteful. Eventually people want to improve this land and **restore** it so it becomes a useful and attractive place. The Park Lane site at Wednesbury is being developed by the private company Triplex Lloyd plc (A–D).

Land use key

- school and playing fields
- mainly housing
- reclaimed land
- open space
- major roads

Diverted River Tame

B *Photosketch of the Park Lane site*

1 Study air photo A and its photosketch B.

  a Shade in the land use on a copy of the photosketch.
  Make sure you use the same shading in the key as on the photosketch.

  b What are the attractions of the site for a business? Think about:
  - access ● employees ● space

18

£50 million Park Lane Development

This major regeneration project at Wednesbury, adjacent to one of the busiest stretches of motorway in the world, will provide industrial/business space, a retail park, homes, a public house and a fast food outlet. It is anticipated that more than 1 000 jobs may result from the completion of the development . . . . The first 250 jobs were created by the opening in January 1991 of the new IKEA furniture store . . . construction work started on the reclamation of this previous industrial tip site in May 1990 . . . redistribution and levelling of 350 000 tonnes of soil, diverting a 620 metre section of the River Tame, construction of 1 100 metres of road and four roundabouts . . . . The award of £3.5 million of City Grant from the Black Country Development Corporation . . . .
Compulsory purchase proceedings have been concluded by the Black Country Development Corporation to provide the last remaining parcels of land required for the construction of a loop road access providing a direct link to Junction 9 of the M6 by April 1992.

▲ C All systems go!

2 Read a description of the Park Lane development in C. Look at photo D.
   a What was the site originally used for?
   b How has the site been changed so far?
   c What is planned for the site?
   d Do you think it will be an improvement?
   e How could local people benefit?
   f Suggest reasons why local people might be unhappy about the development.

D Demolition of factories on the Park Lane site

Living in France

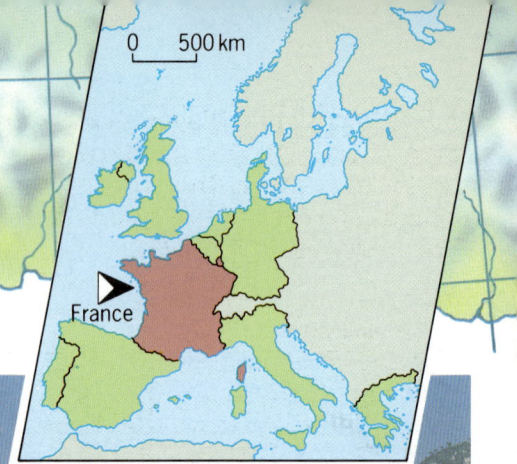

France is one of the main EC countries, measured by size, number of people and wealth. The **population density** map (A) shows where people live. About 74% of the population live in **urban** areas (B). Other people are widely scattered in **rural** areas (C).

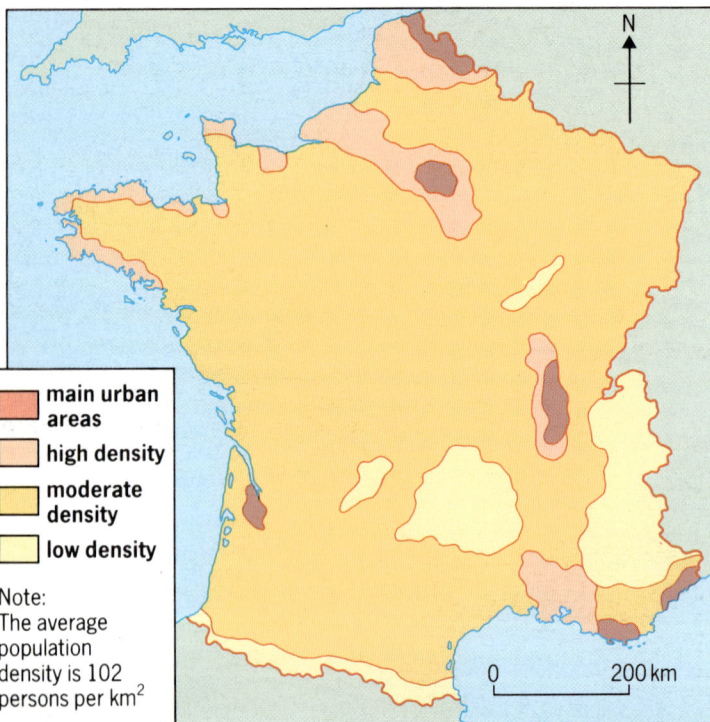

A Population density in France

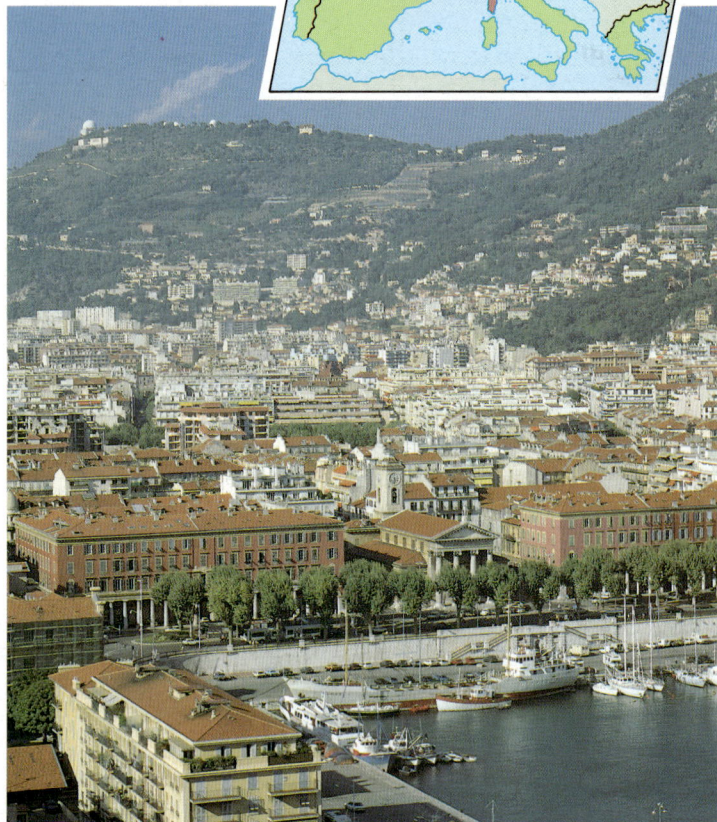

Legend:
- main urban areas
- high density
- moderate density
- low density

Note:
The average population density is 102 persons per km²

N

0   200 km

B *Nice, on the south coast of France*

0   500 km

France

C *The landscape near the Dordogne river in south-west France*

1 Examine map A.
  a Explain what 'population density' means.
  b How would you describe the population density over most of France?
  c Which type of area has the highest population density?
  d Why do you think some areas have a low population density? Use an atlas to help you.

2 Look at photos B and C.
  For each photo, write down what you can tell about:
  ● where the place is
  ● whether the area is urban or rural
  ● the population density
  ● what people do for a living.

Cities, towns and villages all exist to serve a need (D). One need they meet is to act as centres where people can come to buy goods and other services (E, F and G).

D The main cities in France

- **Paris** (pop. 8 510 000)
- **Lyon** (pop. 1 170 000)
- **Marseilles** (pop. 1 080 000)
- **Lille** (pop. 935 000)
- **Bordeaux** (pop. 628 000)
- **Toulouse** (pop. 523 000)
- **Nantes** (pop. 370 000)
- **Nice** (pop. 449 000)
- **Toulon** (pop. 410 000)
- **Rouen** (pop. 380 000)

Note:
- There are 18 more cities with populations over 200 000

F The town of Roanne on the River Loire

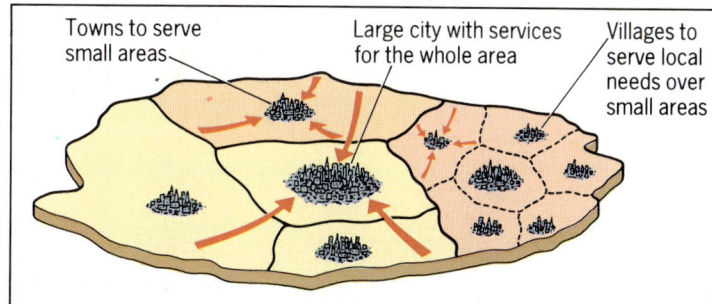

Towns to serve small areas

Large city with services for the whole area

Villages to serve local needs over small areas

G Settlements and their surrounding areas

E A village in Normandy

3 Look at the list of main cities in D. Add the names of the cities onto an outline map of France.

4 Photo F shows the town of Roanne.
   a List the shops and services you can see.
   b What other evidence is there that this is a town centre?
   c How could you tell that it is not a large city?

5 Look at photo E.
   What kinds of goods and services would you expect to find in a village like this?

6 Study diagram G.
   How does this diagram help explain the difference in shops and services between large and small settlements?

The Ile de France region

The Ile de France is the most successful region for business in France (A). The Paris **conurbation** lies at the heart of this region (B). This conurbation is an urban area where several towns have grown into each other (C).

2%	of the area of France
19%	of the population of France
22%	of all jobs in France
27%	of the wealth produced in France

A *Key statistics for the Ile de France*

B *Satellite image of the Paris conurbation*

Colour	Land use
red	parks
dark green/dark red	woods
rectangles of red/pale grey	fields
black	rivers and lakes
blue/grey	buildings
white lines	roads/airports

1 Use the figures in A to prove that the Ile de France region has been successful for business.

2 Study the satellite image B.
 a Measure the size of the built up area from north to south and from east to west.
 b Use an atlas. How has the shape of the land (the **relief**) of the area helped the city to grow? How is the land used outside the city?

	city centre
	inner suburbs
	outer suburbs
	extent of built-up area

Note: Boundaries of these areas are simplified

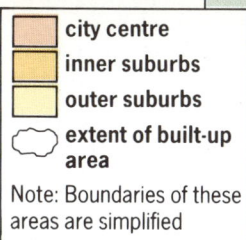

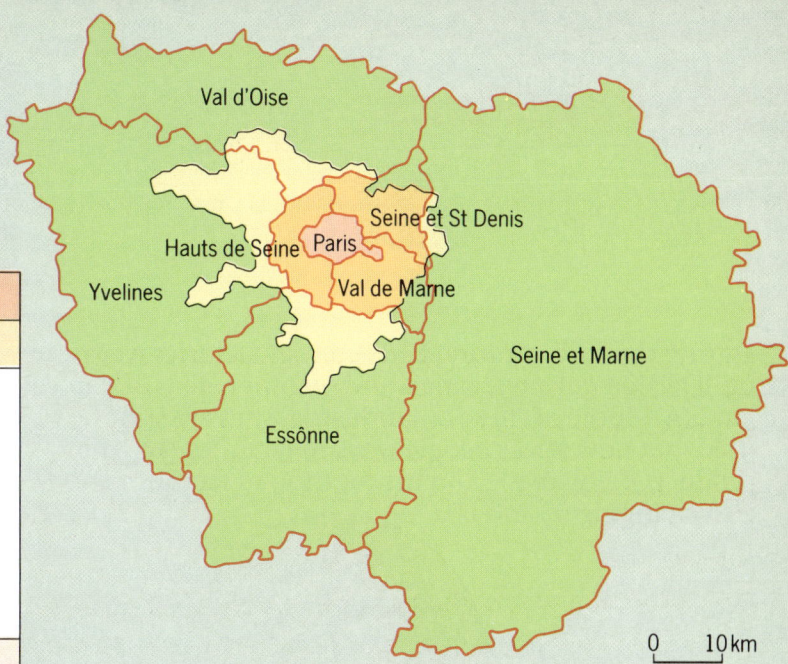

C *Population change in the Paris conurbation*

District	Population in '000	
	1975	**1990**
Paris	2 300	2 147
Hauts de Seine	1 439	1 391
Seine et St Denis	1 322	1 382
Val de Marne	1 216	1 218
Seine et Marne	756	1 075
Yvelines	1 082	1 306
Essônne	923	1 084
Val d'Oise	841	1 048
Total	9 879	10 650

▼D *Scene near the centre of Paris*

▼E *New housing and industry at Cercy-Pontoise on the north-west fringe of the Paris conurbation*

3 Study the figures for population change in C.
  a List the districts by name.
    Work out the population change for each district.
    Put a + or − by each figure, on your list.
  b Use C to describe:
    • where the population has increased
    • where the population has decreased.

4 Photos D and E show areas of Paris.
  Say where these parts of the Paris conurbation are.

What differences can you see in the buildings and land use in the photos?

5 Do you think the city should be allowed to grow outwards any further? Explain your answer. Here are some ideas:
  • travel distance to the centre
  • use of the countryside
  • urban pollution
  • other problems.

Working Paris

During the 19th century, Paris grew as factories were built beside railways, canals and on other areas of flat land (A). Some of these old industrial sites are still used, but now fewer people work in factories (B). The products being made and the location of factories are also changing (C and D).

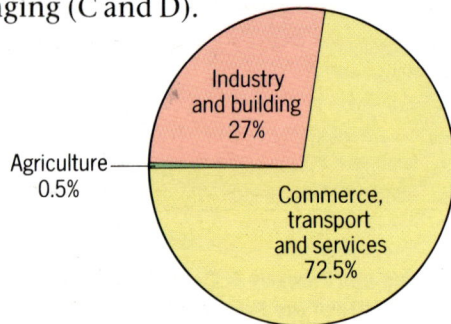

A *Port Autonome de Paris, industrial land along the River Seine*

▲ B *Employment figures for the Ile de France region*

	1979		1987	
	% of total factories	Number employed	% of total factories	Number employed
Metals	12	51 000	6	25 800
Electronics	12	47 900	5	28 200
Precision instruments	2	6 400	3	4 500
Food and drink	4	18 000	8	14 600
Chemicals	8	31 800	3	27 900
Textiles	15	61 600	24	43 600
Furniture	2	6 600	4	4 300
Printing	18	71 400	19	59 900
Other	4	14 600	6	10 700
Construction	23	90 700	22	64 400
Total		400 000		283 900

C *Changes to manufacturing industry in Paris*

D *A new business centre for offices and hi-tech manufacturing in the new town of Marne-la-Vallée*

1 Look at photo A.
   a What use is being made of this industrial land?
   b Give reasons why this use is suitable.
   c What problems might there be for factories located near the centre of Paris?
   d What problems might be caused by factories near the city centre?

2 Study the figures in B and C.
   What do these figures tell you about employment in manufacturing in Paris? In your answer, include:
   • the percentage of people who work in manufacturing
   • examples of products that are increasing and decreasing in production.

3 Use photo D to answer these questions.
   a Describe the location of this business centre.
   b What kinds of business might locate there? Give reasons for your answer.

Service jobs are in shops, offices, and entertainment. Many service jobs are in central Paris where there is easy access for workers and customers (E). Being close together also makes it easier for firms to do business with each other.

Some international firms have their headquarters in Paris. They need good access to other parts of France and to other countries (F). The cost of office space also needs to be considered (H).

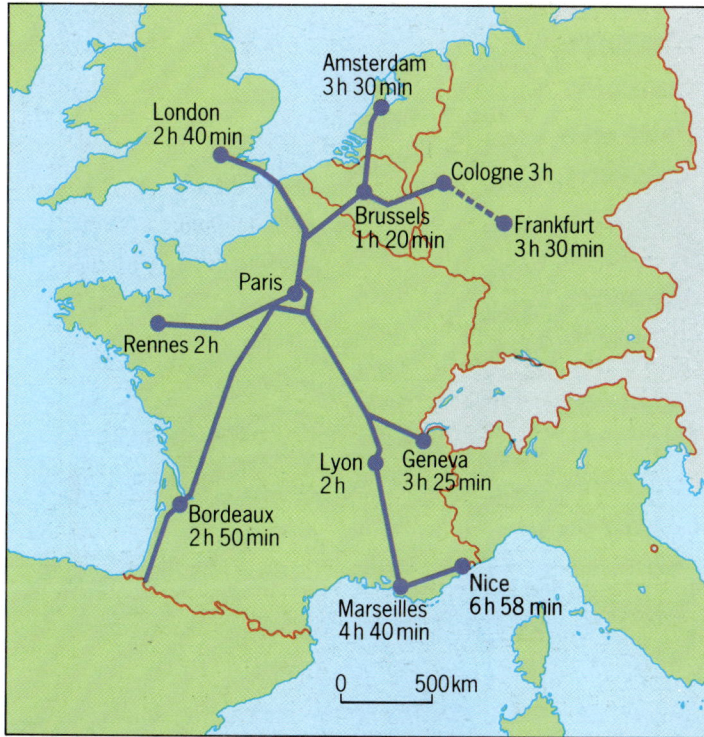

E *A new office centre at La Défense, to the west of the main Paris city centre*

F *Future high speed rail times from Paris*

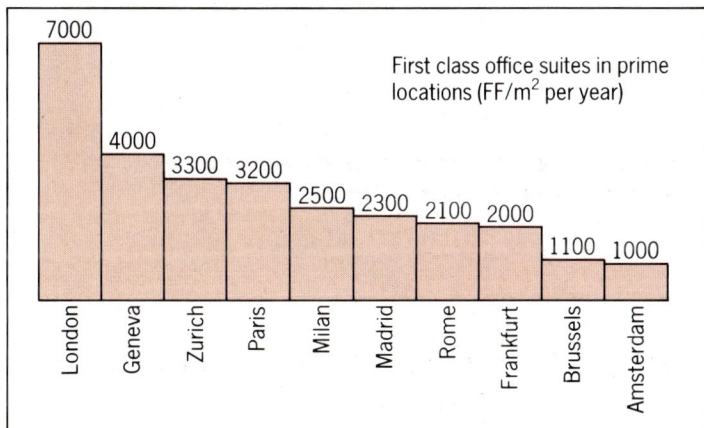

London 2 h 40 min
Amsterdam 3 h 30 min
Cologne 3 h
Brussels 1 h 20 min
Frankfurt 3 h 30 min
Paris
Rennes 2 h
Lyon 2 h
Geneva 3 h 25 min
Bordeaux 2 h 50 min
Marseilles 4 h 40 min
Nice 6 h 58 min
0   500 km

4 With a friend look at photo E. Discuss what you think it would be like to work in La Défense.
5 Study E–H and an atlas map of cities in Europe. Suggest reasons why Paris might be a suitable place for the office headquarters of an international business. Include details of distances, times, places and costs in your answer.

Making cars	**26%**
Service jobs	**30%**
High technology industries	**35%**
Company headquarters	**38%**
Research jobs	**50%**
Insurance company headquarters	**70%**
Bank headquarters	**96%**

G *Industry and commerce in the Ile de France region as percentages of the whole of France*

Success in attracting new jobs to Paris affects other regions of France (G). This is because it is hard to get businesses to move away from Paris when there are so many advantages in being there.

6 Read and think about the figures in G. Use these figures to explain how the business success of Paris can cause problems elsewhere.

7000
4000
3300 3200
2500 2300 2100 2000
1100 1000

First class office suites in prime locations (FF/m^2 per year)

London
Geneva
Zurich
Paris
Milan
Madrid
Rome
Frankfurt
Brussels
Amsterdam

H *The cost of office space*

LONDON BOROUGH OF HAVERING
SACRED HEART OF MARY GIRLS SCHOOL UPMINSTER

Plans for the region

Population predictions
1990–2015 (in '000)

1990	10 380
2000	10 565
2015	10 825

- Predictions vary for the year 2015 between 9 900 and 11 650
- About 50 000 houses will need to be built each year to meet the demand

In the future, space will be needed for more houses, recreation, transport, industry and offices (A).

1. With a partner, look at map A and the figures. Now discuss questions a–b.
   a What do these figures tell you about the future need for housing in Paris?
   b What other demands on space will there be as the city grows?

These demands for space must be met in a way that is properly planned for the whole region (B – F). Some old buildings can be knocked down but others need to be conserved to keep the city's historic character.

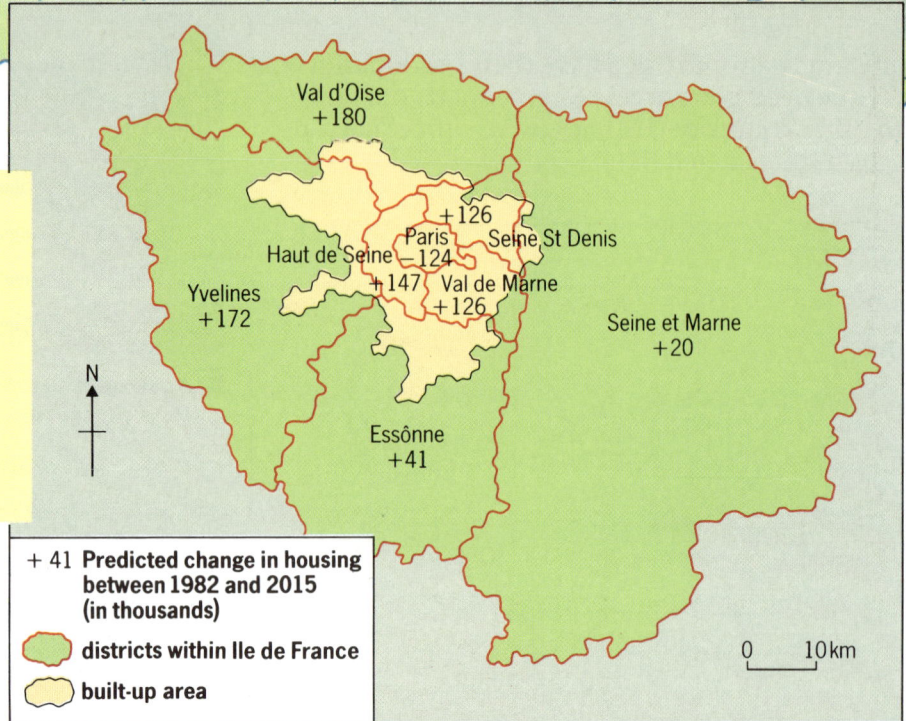

+ 41 **Predicted change in housing between 1982 and 2015 (in thousands)**

districts within Ile de France

built-up area

A *Future demand for housing in Paris*

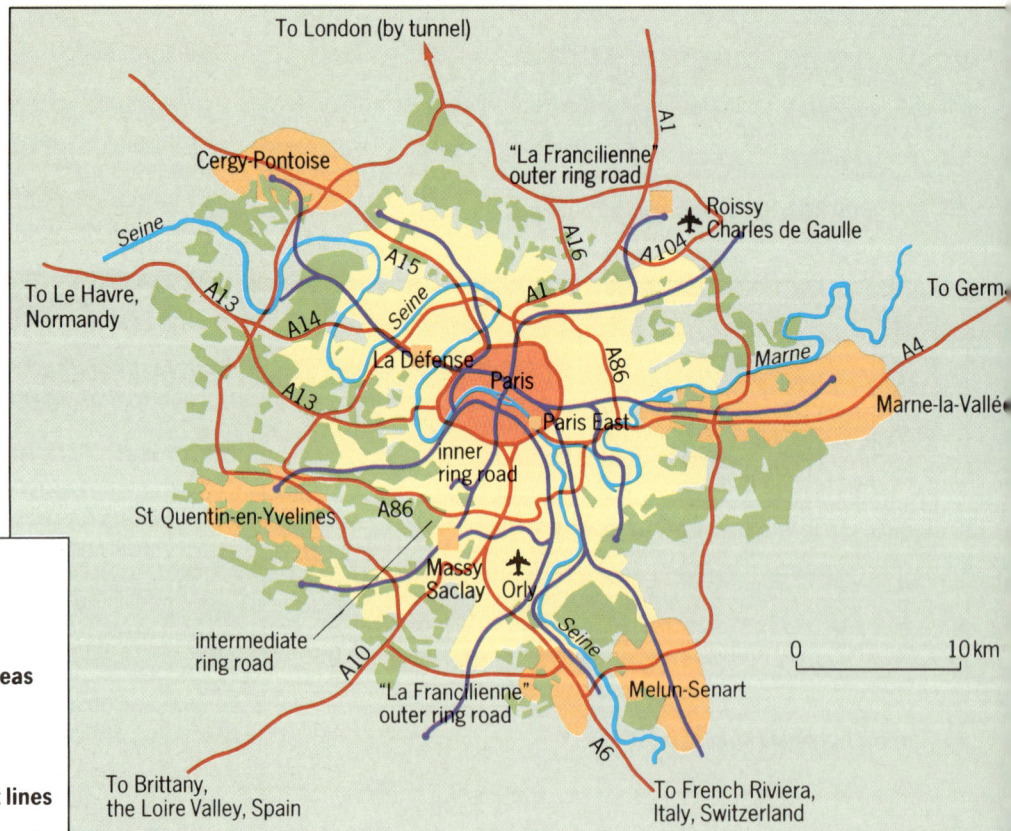

City of Paris

new towns and strategic projects

other urbanized areas

green areas

freeways

major rapid-transit lines

B *Structure plan for the growth of Paris*

- The new Charles de Gaulle international airport with industry, hotels and offices
- Five new towns to house up to 200 000 people in each and give space for factories and offices
- Inner, intermediate and outer ring roads to take traffic out of the city centre
- New hi-tech industries on a site at Massy-Saclay
- New office centres at La Défense and Paris East
- A Regional Rapid Transit system with metro, commuter trains and bus routes linked
- 118 000 hectares of green belt and park areas with Eurodisneyland (a Walt Disney land) at Marne-la-Vallée
- Redevelopment of old inner city industrial sites

▲ **C** *Key features of the Paris structure plan*

2 Study figures B – F.
  a Name the five new towns being built around Paris.
  b What problems will these new towns help to solve?
  c How is some road traffic being kept out of the city centre?
  d What is being built to keep Paris as a centre for office work?
  e Which development will help meet people's leisure needs?

3 Imagine you work for a construction company that builds roads, houses, industrial buildings etc. Choose one of the new types of development taking place in and around Paris. Write a report to describe what you would build. Include maps and sketches to show what your plan would look like and where it would be.

▲ **D** *Building new roads near La Défense office complex*

E *The new Charles de Gaulle airport*

F *New flats built at Marne-la-Vallée new town*

The Brittany coast

Brittany
N
France
0   250 km

The Brittany region is a peninsula with a coastline 3 400 km long (A–C). The coastal areas are called the Armor. The coastline plays an important part in how people earn a living and where settlements are located (D–E).

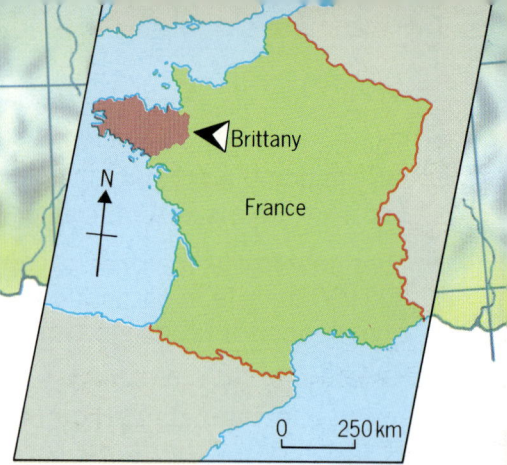

Physical geography report

- Rocks are mainly ancient and hard granites and sandstones.
- The interior was once a mountain range. Now it is worn down to ridges up to 1000 metres high.
- Weathering and erosion have given a rugged coastline with cliffs, sandy bays and estuaries.
- After the last Ice Age, the sea level rose and flooded up the valleys. Long winding estuaries called **rias** were formed.
- In the south, lagoons have been formed behind sand and shingle spits.

▲ **A** *The physical geography of Brittany*

▲ **B** *The Cap Sizun headland and bird reserve in the west of Brittany*

C *A ria inlet near St Malo*

1 Read the information in A and look at photos B and C.
   a Draw a sketch of each photo.
   b Use information from A to add labels to your sketches.

Employment	% figures	
	Brittany	France
Farming/fishing	14	7
Building	7	6
Industry	19	25
Commerce	12	11
Services	48	51

▲ **D** *Employment figures for Brittany*

English Channel

Gulf of St Malo

Roscoff

Morlaix

St Malo

Rance estuary tidal power station

Brest

St Brieuc

Fougeres

Douarnenez

Rennes

Quimper

Concarneau

Lorient

Vannes

✗ ship building and repair

⬛ commercial port

car ferry port

Ⓕ fishing port

Ⓝ naval port

▲ **E** *Main settlements in Brittany*

▲ **F** *Oyster beds near St Malo*

◀ **H** *Brittany Ferries' logo*

Brittany Ferries
The Holiday Fleet

G *A tourist beach near Carnac on Brittany's south coast*

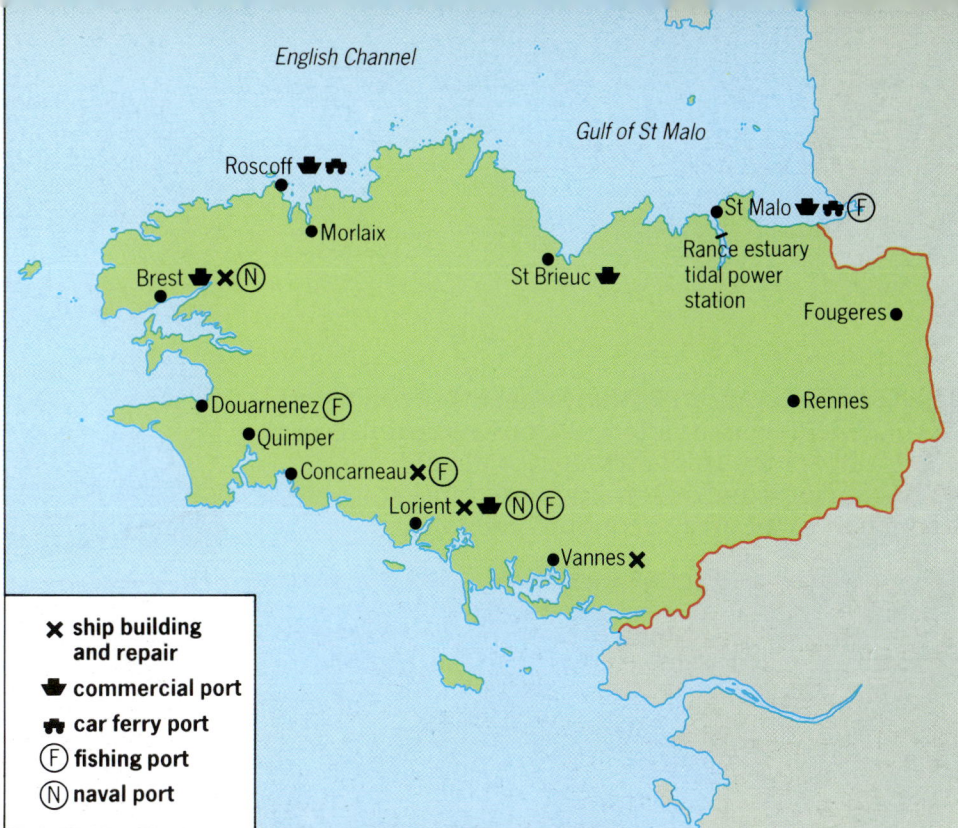

▲ **I** *The yacht marina and old walled town at St Malo*

2 Look at table D.
  a Choose and draw a suitable type of graph to show the figures for employment in Brittany.
  b How are the figures for Brittany different from the French average?

3 Use map E and photos F–G and I to help explain why most large settlements in Brittany are on the coast.

Brittany farmers

The farm landscape in Brittany is mainly a patchwork of small fields with a variety of crops and animals (A, B and C). In France, this landscape is called *bocage*. A good climate is one reason why agriculture still plays a major part in the area's economy (D and E).

▲ **A** *A small dairy herd*

B *Bales of straw after the wheat harvest*

C *Experiments to grow better maize*

Month	J	F	M	A	M	J	J	A	S	O	N	D
Temperature (°C)	7	7	8	11	13	16	17	18	16	13	10	8
Rainfall (mm)	87	75	62	62	47	50	50	55	57	90	105	110

D *Climate figures for Brittany*

E *Farm produce from Brittany* ▷

% of French production
45% of pork
25% of veal (calf)
22% of milk
42% of fishing

1 Use photos A, B and C to answer these questions.
   a What crops and animals can you see? List them.
   b Use details from the photos to describe the features of a *bocage* landscape.
   c Do you find this landscape attractive to look at? Try to explain your answer.

2 Climate figures D will help you to answer the following questions.
   a Grass and most crops do not grow when temperatures are below 6°C.
   How many months are too cold for crops to grow unprotected in Brittany?
   b Most crops need rain throughout the year, though not too much when they are ripening. Cattle also need to have something to eat all year.
   What do you think a farmer might say about rainfall in Brittany?

The mild winter and early spring mean that vegetables can be grown early in the year. These early vegetables are called *primeurs* (F, G and H). Much of the produce is sent to Paris. Some is exported to the UK and even to the USA.

F *Brittany Prince brand vegetables*

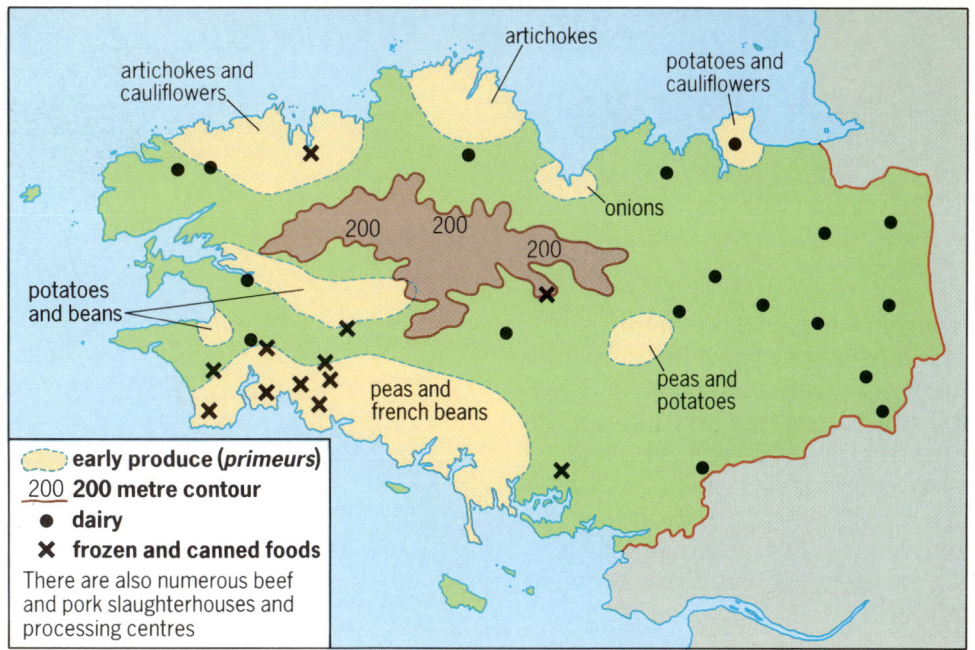

G *Farm produce from Brittany*

Map labels: artichokes and cauliflowers; artichokes; potatoes and cauliflowers; onions; potatoes and beans; peas and french beans; peas and potatoes; 200 metre contours

Key:
- early produce (*primeurs*)
- 200 200 metre contour
- ● dairy
- ✕ frozen and canned foods

There are also numerous beef and pork slaughterhouses and processing centres

3 Study photo F and map G.
  a Explain what *primeurs* are.
  b Why is it important to get these types of crop to a market quickly?
  c Use an atlas map. How long do you think it would take a lorry to travel from St Malo to Paris? (The lorry would average about 60 km/h.)
  d How do you think *primeurs* are sent to the UK and the USA?

Brittany key farming statistics		
	1979	**1988**
Cereals (ha.)	412 600	449 500
Grazing land (ha.)	1 017 700	836 700
Cows	1 391 900	1 152 200
Pigs	4 897 300	6 183 000
Number of farm owners	118 600	92 600

Note: ha. is the abbreviation for hectares, 1 ha. = 10 000 m^2

I *Farm change in Brittany*

One aim of **EC policies** is to make farms more efficient and profitable. The result of this has been that many of the smallest farms have been sold to become part of larger farms (I). Prices paid to farmers for many foods are now set by the EC. This is to make sure farmers produce the amounts that are needed. Some farmers now work together as co-operatives to help sell their produce.

4 With a partner, study figures I.
  a Imagine you lived on a farm in Brittany between 1979 and 1988. Discuss with your partner the main ways in which your farm might have changed. Mention:
  ● what you produce
  ● farm buildings and machinery
  ● how produce is sold.
  b Would you like to make your future in farming in Brittany?
  Give reasons for your answer.

H *Vegetables growing near St Malo*

Hi-tech Brittany

Twenty years ago, lack of jobs forced people to leave Brittany. Jobs in farming were being lost. Manufacturing industry did not want to move to a region on the fringe of France where access was difficult. Now the situation has changed (A). Brittany is getting a new image as hi-tech firms move in (B, C and D).

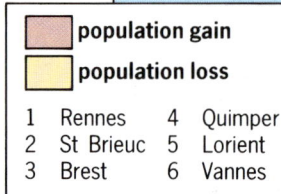

A *Population changes in Brittany, 1975–82*

▨	population gain		
▨	population loss		

1	Rennes	4	Quimper
2	St Brieuc	5	Lorient
3	Brest	6	Vannes

1 Study map A.
   a What is the link between population change and jobs?
   b What do you notice about the size of the area where the population has increased?
   c Which parts of Brittany are still losing population from **migration**? Suggest why.

B *The Brittany logo*

D *Aerial view of the Rennes Atalante Beaulieu industrial site*

METEO FRANCE
Research into weather and weather at sea.

Cedre
Centre for research into marine pollution

TELECOM BRETAGNE
Research into telecommunications

Ideatique
Maintenance of electronic equipment

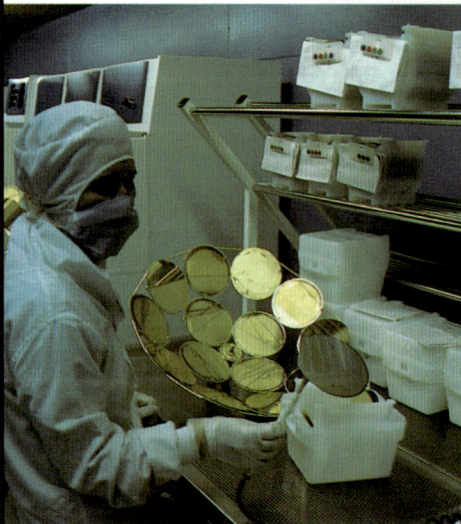

C *Hi-tech firms in Brittany and what they do*

E *A hi-tech worker in the SGS Thompson microelectronics factory*

2 Figure B is Brittany's logo. What do you think the logo is trying to say about Brittany's new image?

3 Look at the information in figures C, D and E.
   a What are hi-tech industries?
   b Give examples of how hi-tech industries can be linked to farming and the sea.

G ***Hi-tech industries, research and communications in Brittany***

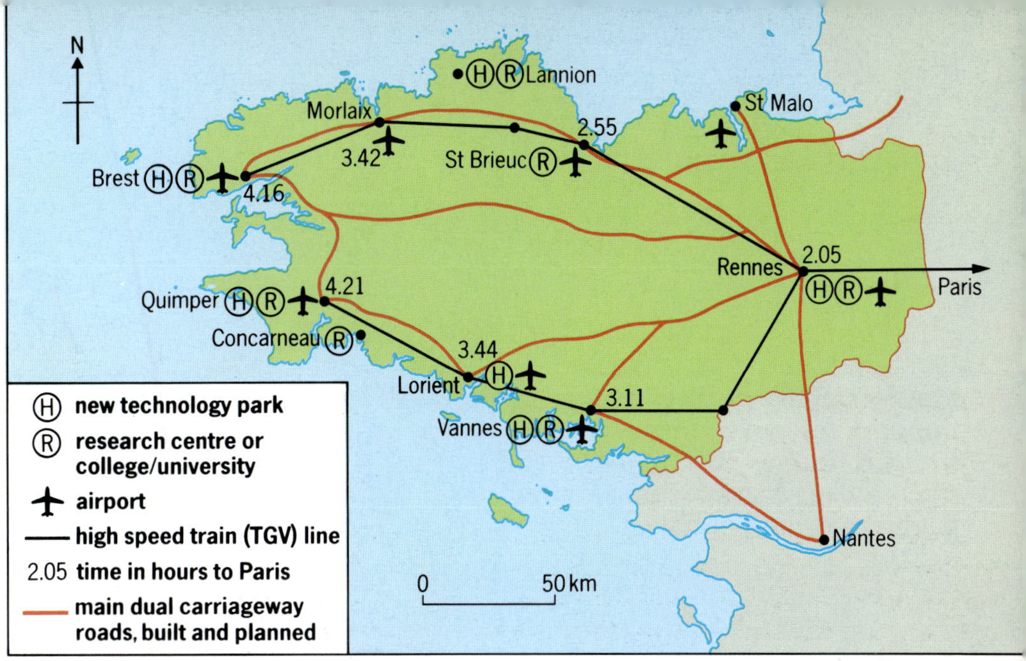
N
Lannion
Morlaix
St Malo
2.55
3.42
St Brieuc
Brest
4.16
2.05
Rennes
Paris
Quimper
4.21
Concarneau
3.44
Lorient
3.11
Vannes
Nantes
new technology park
research centre or college/university
airport
high speed train (TGV) line
2.05 time in hours to Paris
main dual carriageway roads, built and planned
0
50 km

F ***Advantages of Brittany for hi-tech industries***

- Firms not tied to special locations by the need for bulky raw materials
- Improved road, rail and air access
- Research at universities and colleges in the area
- Government grants to help new firms
- Low cost land
- Presence of other firms in the same kind of work
- Attractive environment to live in

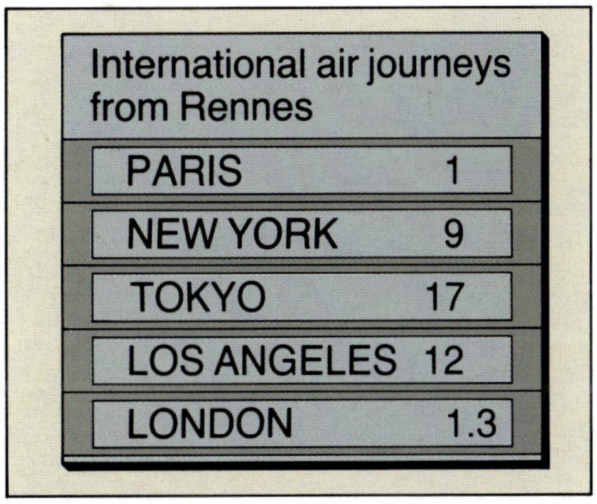
International air journeys from Rennes
PARIS 1
NEW YORK 9
TOKYO 17
LOS ANGELES 12
LONDON 1.3

H ***International air times from Rennes, Brittany, in hours***

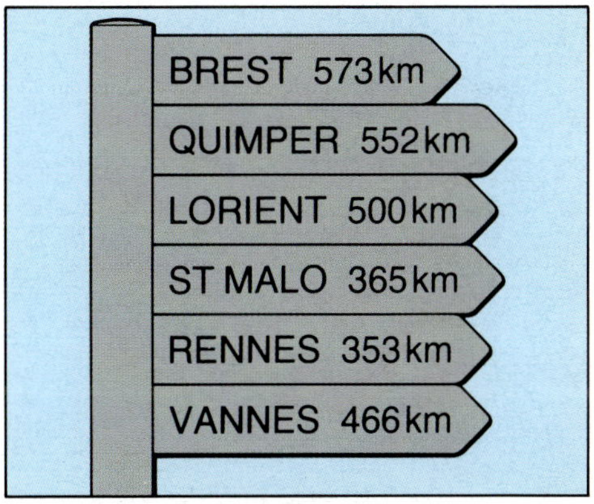
BREST 573 km
QUIMPER 552 km
LORIENT 500 km
ST MALO 365 km
RENNES 353 km
VANNES 466 km

I ***Road distances from Paris to Brittany towns***

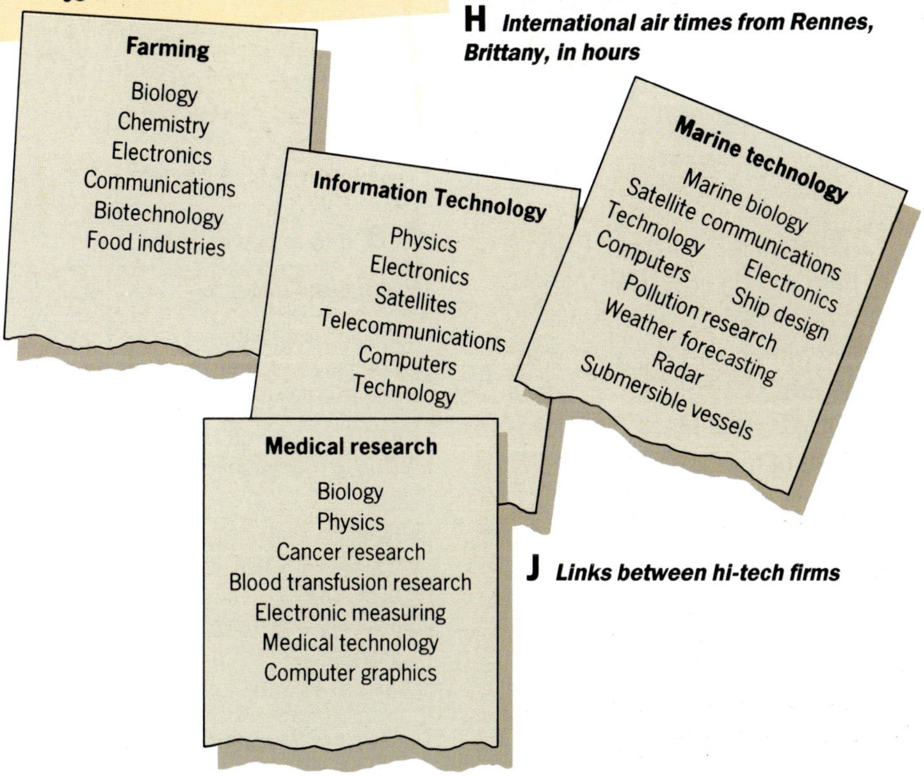
Farming
Biology
Chemistry
Electronics
Communications
Biotechnology
Food industries
Information Technology
Physics
Electronics
Satellites
Telecommunications
Computers
Technology
Marine technology
Marine biology
Satellite communications
Technology
Electronics
Computers
Ship design
Pollution research
Weather forecasting
Radar
Submersible vessels
Medical research
Biology
Physics
Cancer research
Blood transfusion research
Electronic measuring
Medical technology
Computer graphics

J ***Links between hi-tech firms***

4 Study diagrams C and J. Give some examples of how science, electronics, information technology and satellites are used in hi-tech industry.

5 Use the information in C, G, H and I to explain why distance to other parts of France is not a major problem to hi-tech firms who move to Brittany.

6 In a group produce a large advert or booklet to show the attractions of Brittany for hi-tech industries. Include information given in F.

Seeing Italy

Most of us have pictures in our minds of foreign countries. These **mental images** may or may not be true. Collage A shows some images people may have of Italy.

A *Images of Italy*

	Italy	UK
Area	301 000 km^2	245 000 km^2
Population	57 million	57 million
Tourists (per year)	56 million	17 million
Passenger cars	24 million	28 million
Life expectancy	75 years	74 years
Urban population (% of total population)	68	92
Fertilizer used (kg/ha. of agricultural land)	120	147
Tractors in use	1.2 million	1.5 million

▲B *Italy in figures (1990)*

Exports by value (%)	Italy	UK
Food and live animals	5.2	5.2
Beverages and tobacco	1.1	2.4
Raw materials (ores etc)	1.9	2.7
Mineral fuels (oil, gas)	2.8	11.9
Animal and vegetable oil and fats	0.3	–
Chemicals	7.2	13.3
Manufacturing (e.g. textiles, footwear)	47.1	26.9
Machinery and transport equipment	33.6	34.8
Other	0.8	2.8

C *Italy's main exports (1990)*

1 **a** Write down a caption for each image in A.
   b Draw or describe any other images you have of Italy. How did you get these images?

2 In B there is some selected information about Italy, compared to the UK. Copy five pieces of information and, next to each, explain what you think it tells you about Italy.

3 **a** Choose another country in the EC, other than the UK. (Look back to page 5, E, to help you decide). Collect photos or draw sketches to illustrate your images of that country.
   b Discuss your ideas, in pairs or in groups. Are your images:
   ● fair
   ● true
   ● distorted?
   What could you find out to get a better picture?
   c Write a summary of your findings.

D *In and around Italy*

Bari											Distances in kilometres
667	**Bologna**										
720	105	**Florence**									
944	295	227	**Genoa**								
878	210	298	142	**Milan**							
261	592	490	714	785	**Naples**						
692	1313	1211	1435	1506	734	**Palermo**					
457	1078	976	1200	1271	499	235	**Reggio de Calabria**				
449	379	277	501	572	219	940	705	**Rome**			
94	750	803	1027	961	344	626	391	532	**Taranto**		
997	329	395	170	140	882	1593	1368	669	1080	**Turin**	
760	152	254	398	267	741	1462	1227	528	843	402	**Venice**

Example: Rome – Florence = 277 km

▲ E *Distances in Italy, in kilometres*

F *Travel chart*

4 **a** Draw a bar graph of Italy's exports, listed in C.
  b What does your graph tell you about Italy's exports?
  c In pairs, list some Italian products you have seen for sale in your home area.

5 Study and make a copy of map D.
  a Use an atlas to fill in the key on a copy of the map.
  b Shade each country in a different colour.
  c Use your map and atlas to help you complete these sentences:
    Most of Italy is covered with _____.
    Countries 1–4 each have a _____ with Italy. The seas surrounding Italy are all parts of a larger sea called the _____.

6 You are planning a car tour of Italy. These are the things you want to do on your tour:

  • spend 21 days touring
  • start and end at the same city
  • visit each town or city on map D once
  • if possible, travel no more than 200 kilometres on any day
  • stay a few days at cities which are of particular interest to you

  a On an outline map of Italy, mark your route by joining up the towns or cities with a coloured line.
  b Use distance chart E to write down the distances between the places on your route.
  c Complete your tour plan on a copy of chart F.
  d Write a short description of your tour.
    Mention which parts of Italy had shorter stretches between cities, and those parts where the journey was more difficult.
    Your atlas will help you to find extra information.

Patterns and people

A Italy: regions and main cities

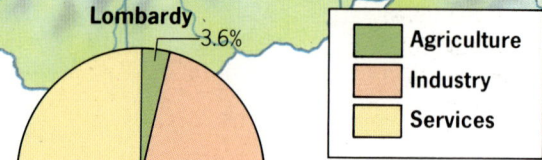

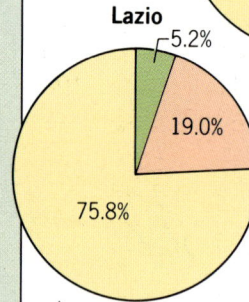

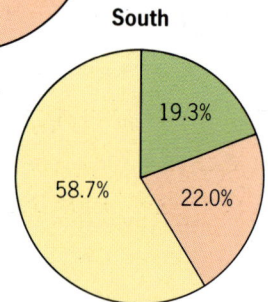

Population of cities
- 2.0 – 3.0 million
- 1.0 – 2.0 million
- 0.5 – 1.0 million

Population of regions to be plotted
- 0.5 million

Map labels: NW, Lo, NE, Milan, Turin, Genoa, ER, C, Rome, L, AM, Naples, C, S, Sa, Palermo, Si

Lombardy — 3.6%, 43.4%, 53.0%

Lazio — 5.2%, 19.0%, 75.8%

South — 19.3%, 22.0%, 58.7%

Legend:
- Agriculture
- Industry
- Services

▲ B The employment structure of the regions

▼ C Populations of the regions

Region	Population in millions	0.5 million dots to be plotted
North-west (NW)	6.25	12
Lombardy (Lo)	8.8	18
North-east (NE)	6.5	13
Emilia-Romagna (ER)	4.0	8
Centre (C)	5.8	12
Lazio (L)	5.1	10
Campania (Ca)	5.7	11
Abruzzi-Molise (AM)	1.6	3
South (S)	6.8	14
Sicily (Si)	5.1	10
Sardinia (Sa)	1.6	3

1   Study map A and population data C.
   a Using C, plot the population of each region in dots representing 0.5 million people onto a copy of map A. Make sure your dots are the same size as in the key.
   b Which two regions are the most densely populated?
   c Is the population of Italy concentrated in a few regions or quite evenly distributed?
   d Which region has the fewest people and is the most thinly populated?

2   Copy and complete the chart on the right using pie charts B.

Description	Name of the region
A high proportion of the people still working in agriculture	
Highly mechanized farming so fewer workers are needed	
Industry employs nearly half the workforce	
Government offices in the capital city and also tourism explain the very high percentage in service industries	

Region	Unemployment rate %	Infant mortality per 1000 births	Gross Domestic Product* per person
North-west (NW)	7.6	8.1	119
Lombardy (Lo)	4.7	8.3	138
North-east (NE)	6.1	7.0	117
Emilia-Romagna (ER)	5.7	8.7	128
Centre (C)	8.1	9.1	111
Lazio (L)	10.6	9.0	118
Campania (Ca)	22.9	12.0	67
Abruzzi-Molise (AM)	10.0	11.3	87
Puglia-Basilicata/Calabria (PBC)	18.4	11.9	68
Sicily (Si)	18.6	12.1	70
Sardinia (Sa)	18.2	10.1	75

* Gross Domestic Product (GDP) is the value of all goods and services produced in a year. The EC average is 100.

▲ D *Contrasts in the quality of life*

By world standards, Italy is a modern, wealthy and developed country. There are regions in Italy, however, which are less developed and where the people have a poorer quality of life.

E *Italy and its regions*

3 Study the data on the regions of Italy, in D.

a On a copy of map E, shade in the unemployment figures for each region. Use the key provided.

b Use your shading to divide Italy into three large regions. Choose a title for each region, from this list:
- Centre ● Islands
- North East ● South East
- South ● Western
- North Centre

c Complete the title boxes on your copy of E.

d In pairs or in a group, write a report expressing your concern at the pattern of inequality shown. The following words may help:
- poorer
- wealthy
- less developed
- better quality of life
- produce more wealth for Italy
- poorer health care and living conditions.

% unemployed
	4.0 – 7.9
	8.0 – 11.0
	18.0 – 23.0

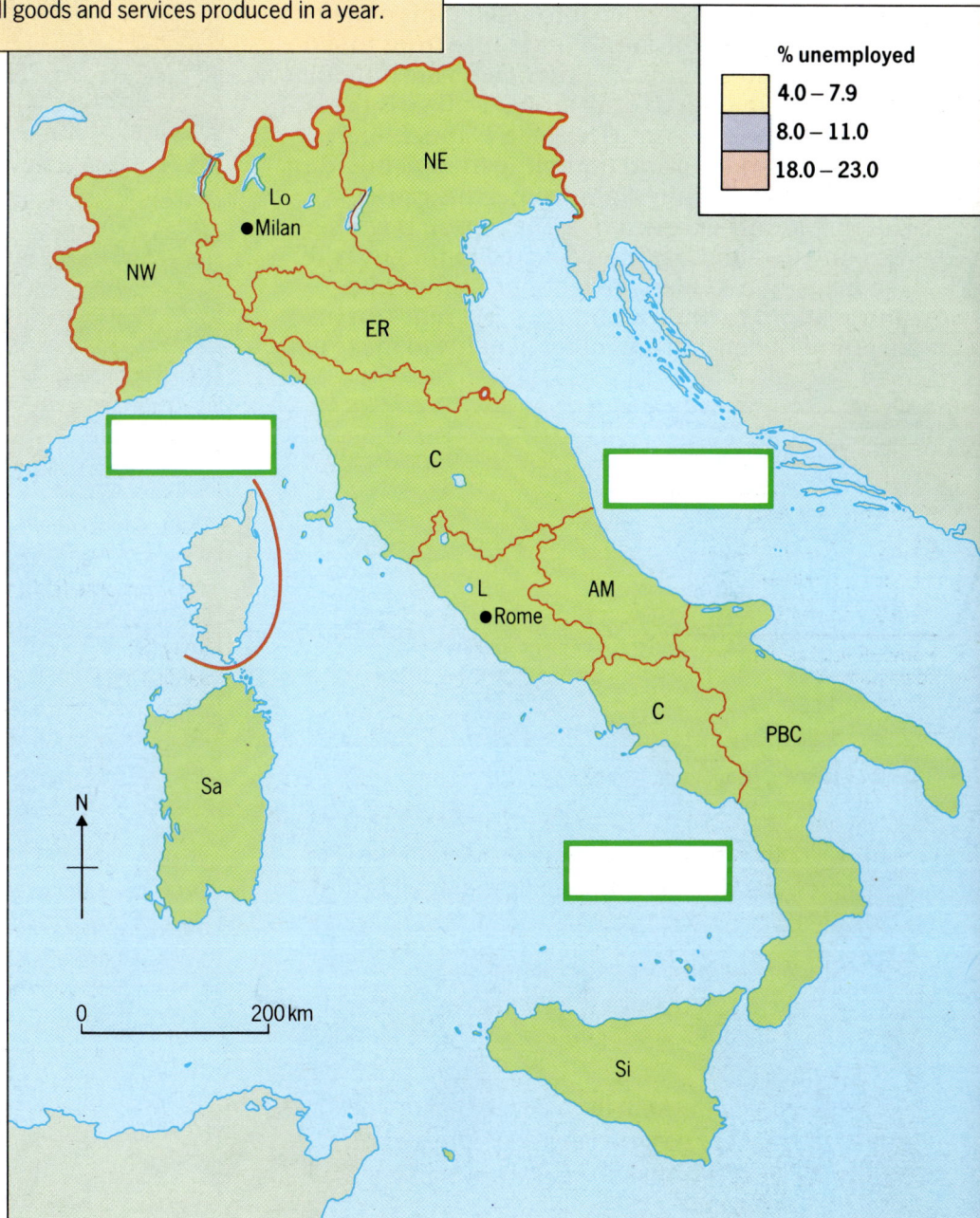

The rural heart of the south

Aliano is like thousands of other villages in the south of Italy. It is perched on a ridge 500 metres above sea level (A). Surrounding it are craggy hills, landslips, gullies and valleys.

The farmer in photo B follows the traditional ways of farming. His donkey carries his loads and pulls his plough. His land is divided into small plots on which he grows food for the family and some crops to sell. Hillsides are steep and the plots of land are difficult to reach. At dawn each day the farmer walks his flock of sheep and goats to graze. The goats wander freely, stripping vegetation and trampling the soil into dust. When the heavy winter rains come, this causes widespread **soil erosion** (D). The topsoil is washed away and the land becomes covered in rough scrub. Like many of his elderly neighbours, this farmer cannot afford to improve his farm. He relies on his government pension and other benefits to make ends meet.

A *Aliano, a hill top village*

B *A local family farmer*

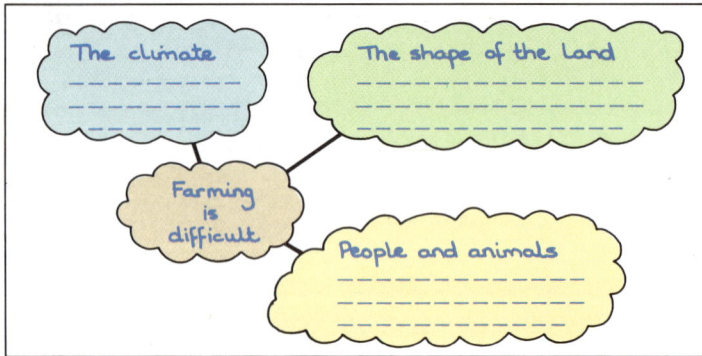

C *Why farming is difficult*

The climate _ _ _ _ _ _ _ _

The shape of the Land _

Farming is difficult

People and animals _

1 Read the text again. Draw up a diagram like C to show the reasons why farming is difficult in this area.

2 Study the land ownership figures in E.
   a Write a summary of what you have found out, including the size of farm which most farmers work.
   b Compare this with the average UK farm of about 80 ha. Why do such very small farms make it difficult for farmers to make a living?

D *Land eroded by animals and rain*

Farm size (ha.)	Number of farms	Area of Aliano covered (ha.)
0–2	112	106
2–5	128	391
5–10	96	657
10–20	62	839
20–50	43	1361
Over 50	33	3911
1 hectare (ha.) = 10 000 m^2		

E *Farms and land in Aliano*

F Simplified map showing land use around Aliano

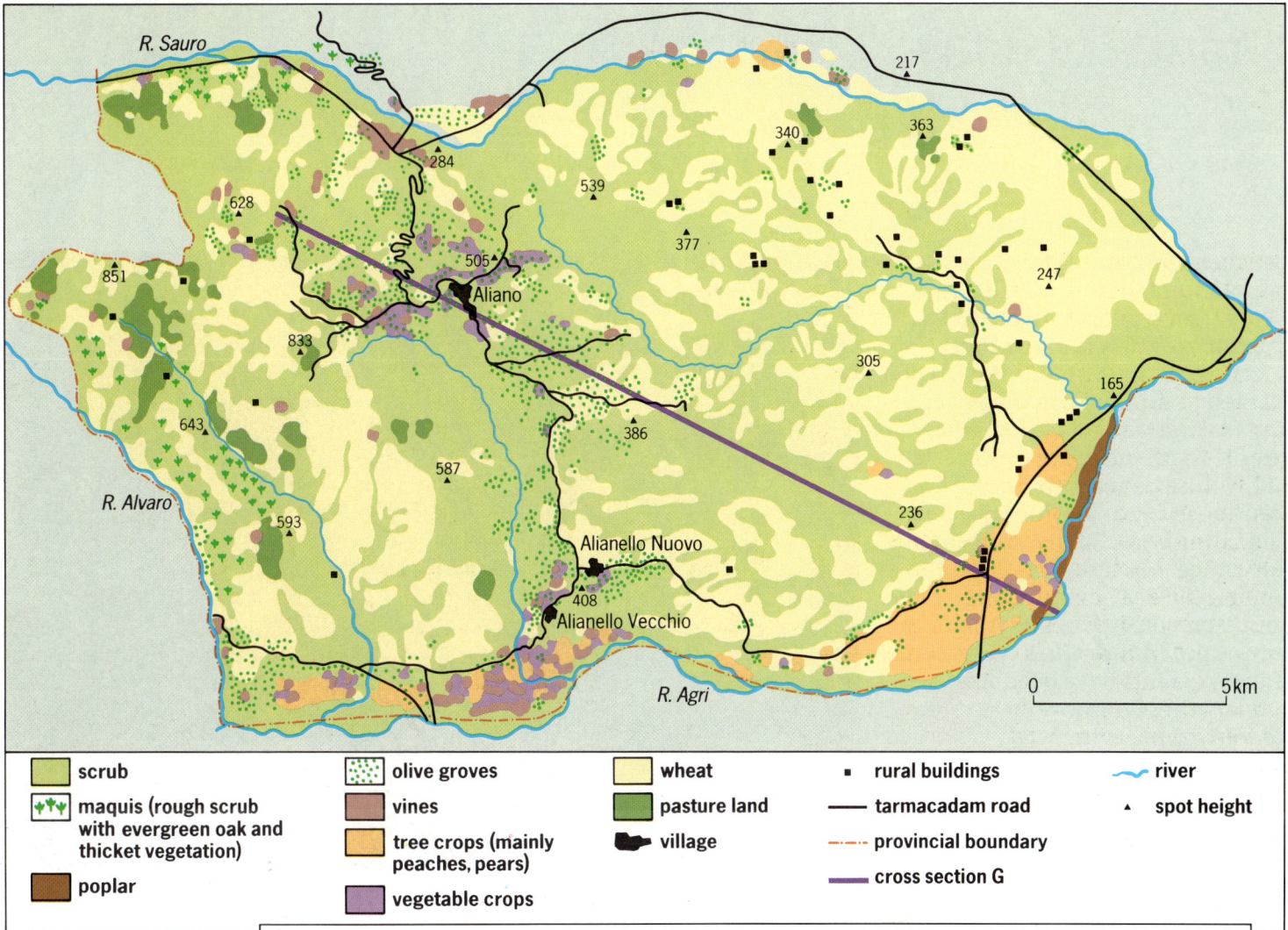

Key:

- scrub
- maquis (rough scrub with evergreen oak and thicket vegetation)
- poplar
- olive groves
- vines
- tree crops (mainly peaches, pears)
- vegetable crops
- wheat
- pasture land
- village
- rural buildings
- tarmacadam road
- provincial boundary
- cross section G
- river
- spot height

Spot heights shown on map: R. Sauro, 217, 363, 340, 284, 539, 628, 505 Aliano, 377, 247, 851, 833, 305, 165, 643, R. Alvaro, 387, 386, 236, 593, Alianello Nuovo, 408 Alianello Vecchio, R. Agri

Scale: 0 — 5km

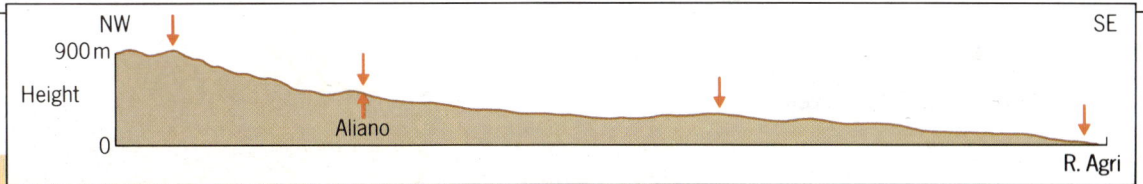

G Cross-section NW to SE in Aliano

(NW) 900 m Height, Aliano, 0, R. Agri (SE)

3

a Use map F and the key to name the two main land uses around Aliano.

b Cross-section G shows the shape of the land along the line on map F. Describe how the farmers make use of the different heights and types of land at the arrows.

c Copy and complete this table. What pattern do you notice? How do you explain this pattern? (Think of the time spent tending different crops.)

	Average distance from Aliano (m)
Orchard crops and olive groves	
Wheat	

d Draw a bar graph to show the major crops listed in H.

e Which of these crops are sown or planted every year? Which are in the fields all year?

Crop	Hectares planted
Wheat	3342
Vegetables (mainly beans)	50
Forage crops (for animals)	119
Olives	519
Vines	118
Fruits (peaches, pears etc.)	129

H Crops in Aliano

Change in Aliano

Between 1952 and 1987 Aliano's population fell from 2297 to 1600. Many young people **migrated** to the north of Italy and to other countries in western Europe. They wanted to escape from the poverty and isolation of village life. Many people in Aliano are over 55 years old. Young people often see farming as hard, unprofitable and degrading work. Many want shop and office jobs but are unemployed. The future for southern villages such as Aliano is uncertain. In the past 30 years some improvements have been made, but will these improvements stop people from leaving?

A People expect a more varied diet than they did years ago. The village now has 11 food shops. Travelling salespeople and the fortnightly market bring in new foods

B The damming of the local Agri and Sauro rivers has resulted in valley land being irrigated. The farms here are intensive and profitable

C The road network has been improved. Faster main roads link Aliano with nearby towns

D Comunita Montana

The government is providing help through a rural planning agency called Comunita Montana. Its aim is to encourage people to stay on the land. It provides 50% of the cost for new buildings, irrigation projects and new livestock. It has linked many farms to the village with tarmac roads. Trees have been planted to reduce soil erosion. The Comunita Montana (photos D) also provides money for people to set up and work in co-operatives

1 Read the text on the left hand page again.
   a Draw a bar graph to show Aliano's change in population between 1952 and 1987. Give the graph a title.
   b Explain why more and more people in Aliano are over 55 years old. What problems do you think this will cause in the area?

2 Using photos D, draw simple labelled sketches to illustrate the work of the Comunita Montana.

3 Imagine you were living in Aliano. Think of all the advantages and disadvantages of living there. Use all the information on these two pages to answer this question: Would you want to stay, or would you leave the village?
   Give reasons for your choice.

Support for the south

Key:
- motorways
- larger areas of lower, flatter land
- major tourist areas
- iron and steel
- mechanical engineering
- plastics
- petrochemicals
- oil refining
- car assembly

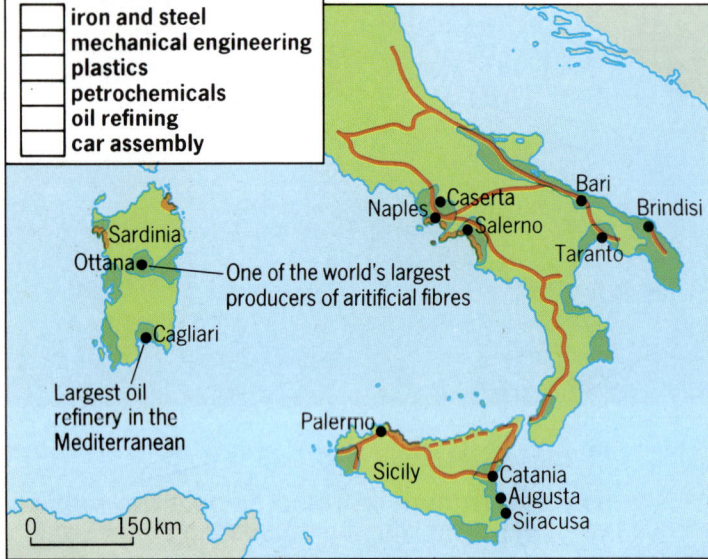

Map locations: Sardinia, Ottana — One of the world's largest producers of artificial fibres, Cagliari, Largest oil refinery in the Mediterranean, Naples, Caserta, Salerno, Bari, Brindisi, Taranto, Palermo, Sicily, Catania, Augusta, Siracusa

0   150 km

A *Industrial centres in southern Italy*

Southern Italy has three times as much unemployment as the north of Italy. The income for most southerners is half the average for the whole of Italy. Over the past 40 years both the EC and the Italian government have **invested** billions of lire in improving the lives of the people in the south.

They have had mixed success. Housing, health and education have improved. Four thousand new factories have been built and 400 000 new jobs have been created. In some areas, new developments have transformed the landscape (D).

Location	Industries
Bari-Brindisi-Taranto	mechanical engineering, petrochemicals, iron and steel
Catania-Augusta-Siracusa	plastics, petrochemicals
Naples-Caserta-Salerno	iron and steel, car assembly

B *The locations of industry*

Features of the location of industries	Naples-Caserta-Salerno	Bari-Brindisi-Taranto	Catania-Augusta-Siracusa
Inland			
Coastal		✓	
Concentrated in a few places		✓	
Evenly distributed in many locations			
On high land			
On lower, flatter land		✓	

C *Where the main industries are found*

D *Saras oil refinery*

1 **a** Make a copy of map A.
      Make up a symbol for each industry and fill in the key.
   b Use chart B to plot these symbols on your map.
   c Complete a copy of chart C by putting ticks in the columns to show where industries are found. An example has been done for you.
   d Look at your results. Write a few sentences to describe where the main industrial areas in the south are found.
   e In what ways is the oil refinery in photo D typical of a southern industrial area?

The 'growth pole' strategy
The government selected areas with large populations, flat land and adequate power supplies. Large industrial plants were built. It was hoped that they would attract other industries which needed their products. More and more jobs would be created.

E *Cathedrals in the desert*

2 Cartoon E will help you to answer questions a–b.
a What is the main criticism that local people may have about the large industrial plants?
b The industrial plants have been described as 'cathedrals in the desert'. Why do you think they have been called this?

3 The Italian government has spent huge amounts of money in improving the **infrastructure** of the south. The infrastructure of an area is its framework of communications, sewerage and water system and power supply. In the south, ports have been modernized, motorways have been built and railways have been electrified.
a How has the infrastructure been improved, as seen in photo F?
b What is an *autostrada*?
c What impresses you about this road?
d Draw a sketch of the photo. Label the main features.

4 Look at cartoon G.
Thousands of tourists take advantage of the *autostrada* and head south.
a Why have the new *autostrada* resulted in more people holidaying in the south?
b What sorts of jobs and businesses will benefit from tourism?

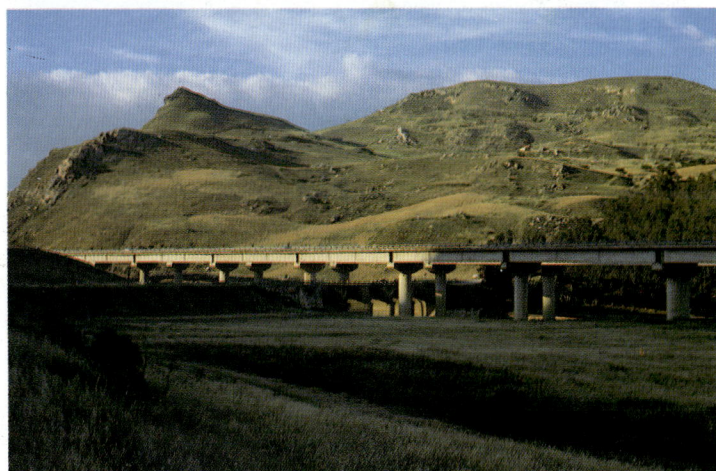

F *Road to the south, a stretch of autostrada*

G *Holiday route south*

The 'golden triangle'

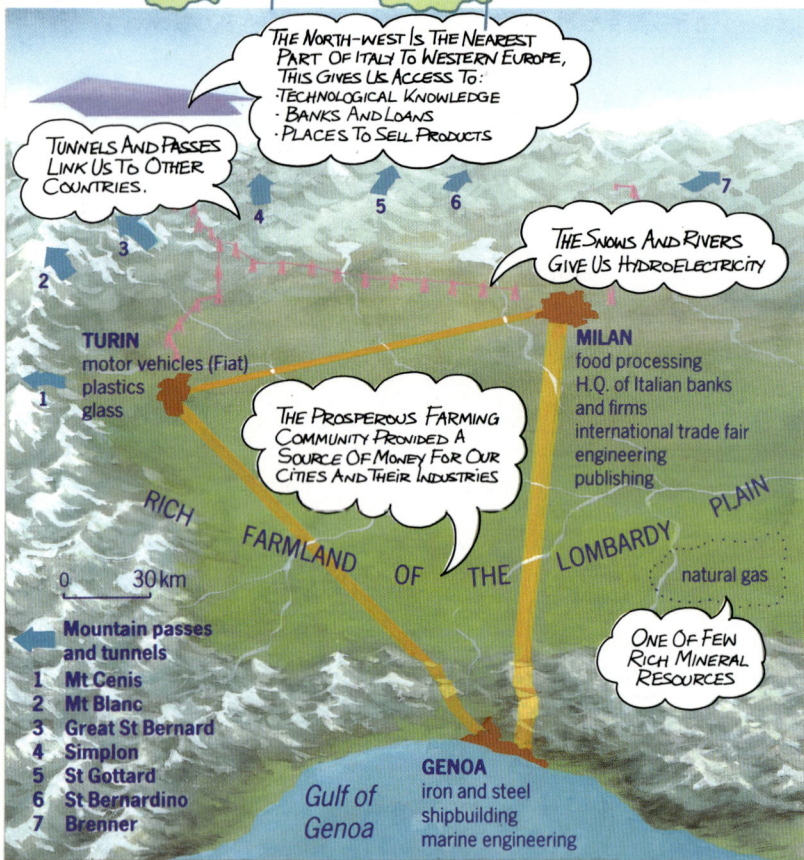

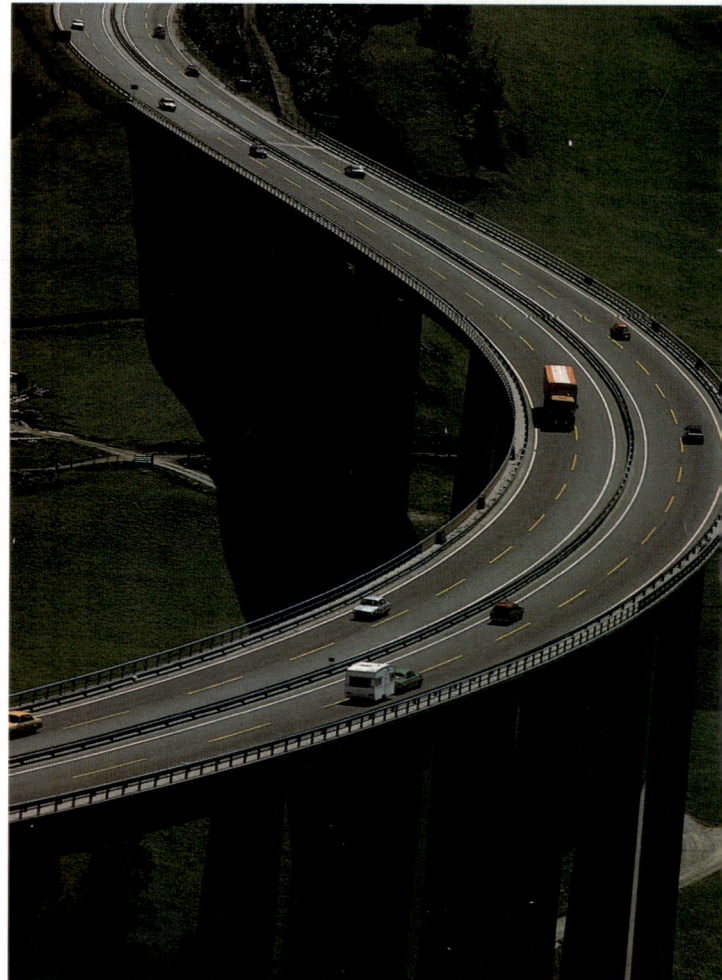

A *North-west Italy and the 'golden triangle'*

The north-west has been the main industrial region of Italy for a long time. It has become the centre for **heavy industries** such as metal and mechanical engineering, chemicals and shipbuilding. It is also important for the car industry.

Industry is concentrated in the 'golden triangle' around Milan, Genoa and Turin. Between 1951 and 1971 the 'golden triangle' attracted thousands of migrant workers from the poorer south.

B *Approaching the Brenner Pass*

---

1 a Study map A.
   Draw a simple sketch map of the region and mark:
   - Milan, Genoa and Turin
   - the 'golden triangle'
   - the coast and mountains
   - the Plain of Lombardy

   b Copy down these three headings and use the handwritten bubbles on A to add notes under each one.
   - Farming
   - Closeness to western Europe
   - Power supplies.

   c Using your notes, explain why the north-west became a major industrial region.

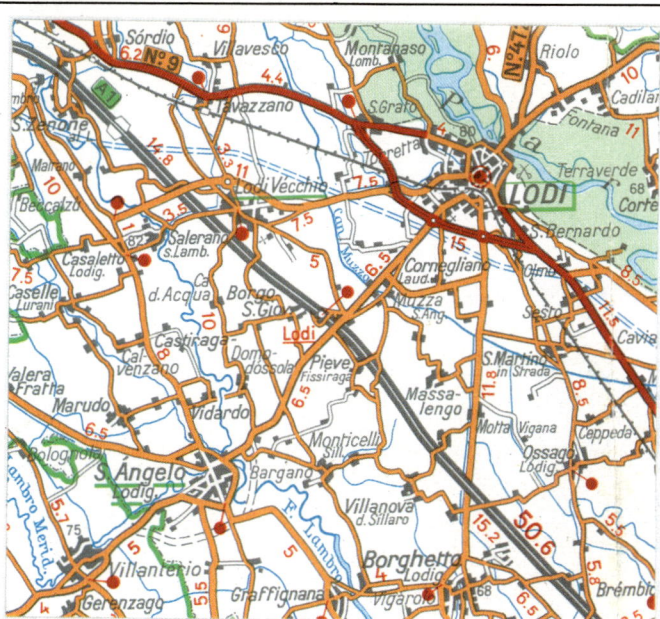

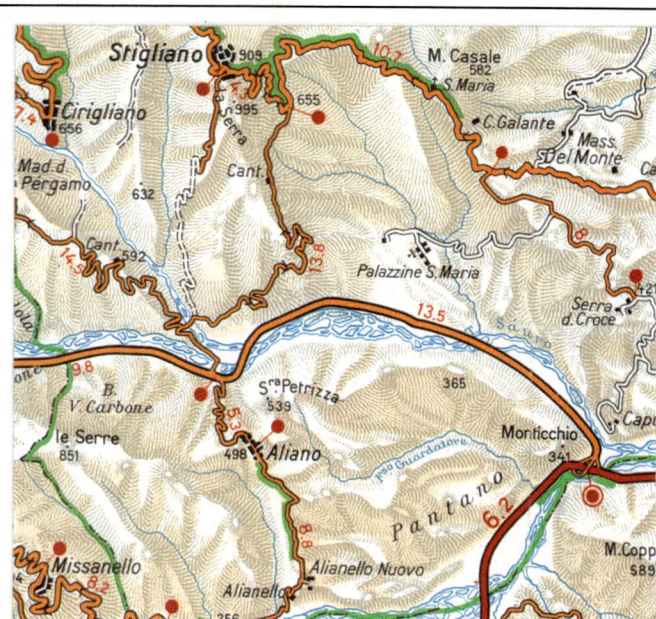

C *Route map of the Lodi area*

D *Route map of the Aliano area*

2 a Draw a photosketch of photo B.
   b Label on the main features of the road and landscape.

3 Study route map C.
   a List the different types of route shown.
   b How dense is the **network** of routes?
   c If you wanted to travel from north to south, how much choice of routes is there?
   d How does the transport network on the map help explain why businesses have been attracted to the north-west?

4 Work in pairs to study map D and key E.
   a Plan a cycle route from Alianello to Stigliano.
   b Draw a sketch map of your route.
   c Describe what you would expect your ride to be like. Mention:
   • the shape of your route
   • the time it might take
   • how easy it would be
   • whether you would pass any villages
   • the type of road you would be on.
   d Why might a managing director be unhappy about setting up a company in this area?

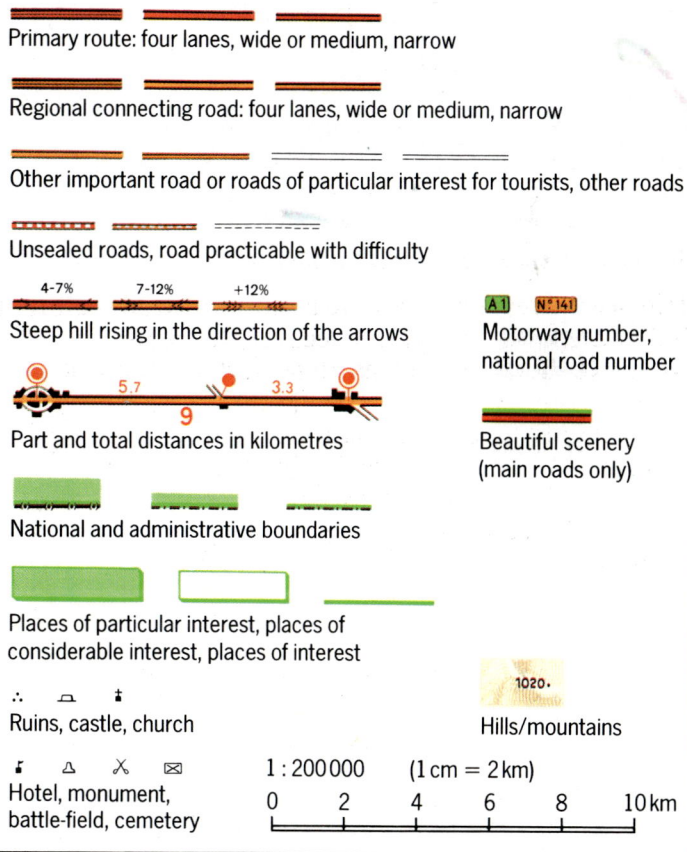

Primary route: four lanes, wide or medium, narrow

Regional connecting road: four lanes, wide or medium, narrow

Other important road or roads of particular interest for tourists, other roads

Unsealed roads, road practicable with difficulty

4-7%   7-12%   +12%
Steep hill rising in the direction of the arrows

A 1   N° 141
Motorway number, national road number

5.7   3.3
9
Part and total distances in kilometres

Beautiful scenery (main roads only)

National and administrative boundaries

Places of particular interest, places of considerable interest, places of interest

∴   ⌂   ⸸
Ruins, castle, church

1020·
Hills/mountains

♪   △   ⚔   ✉
Hotel, monument, battle-field, cemetery

1 : 200 000   (1 cm = 2 km)
0   2   4   6   8   10 km

E *Key to the maps*

Patterns of land use

A *North Italy from space*

Colour	Land use
grey streaks	outwash material
deep red	vegetation
black	water
white	snow
grey-green	urban areas

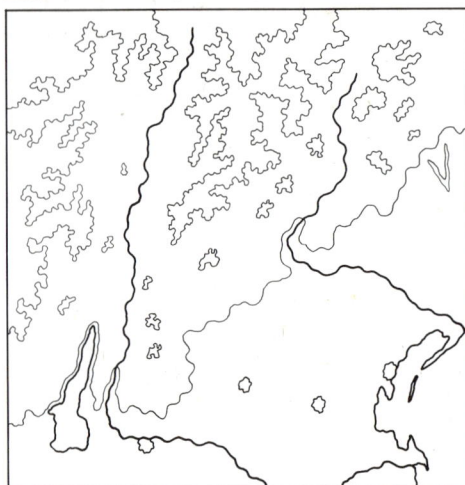

◀B *A simple sketch of satellite image A*

Pictures taken from space give us a distinctive view of the earth. These **satellite images** use false colours. The key in A shows the land use of the satellite photo.

1 Study satellite image A.
  a Make an enlarged copy of sketch B. It has been divided up into different land use areas.
  b Use the satellite image key and an atlas to find the following:
  ● the Plain of Lombardy
  ● the Italian Alps
  ● Lake Garda
  ● the rivers Adige and Piave
  ● the cities of Venice, Verona, Vicenza and Padua
  ● the Adriatic Sea.
  Label them on your sketch map.
  c Colour in your sketch and add a key.
  d Describe the shapes made by the mountains.
  e What difference can you see between the land use and settlement of the mountains and the plain?
  f Explain why they are so different.

2 Imagine you are a member of a company which processes and markets satellite images.
  a Working in pairs, compose a letter describing the many uses for these images.
  b Write down a list of organizations which might be interested in receiving your letter.

The farming systems on the Plain of Lombardy are very different from those of Aliano (pages 38–41). There are both physical and human reasons for the way the land is used in the Plain of Lombardy (D). Diagram C shows how the human and physical influences combine to produce profitable farming on the plain.

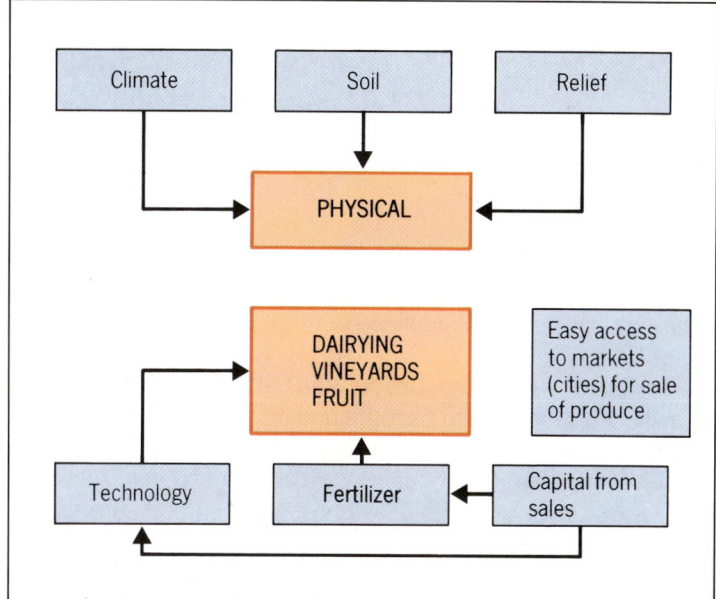

3 **a** Make a copy of diagram C.
    Leave plenty of space in the red boxes to add notes, using the headings in the other boxes.
  b Use the information in A and D, and the Lodi route map C on page 45 to fill in the boxes.
  c Use your answers to help you complete these sentences.
    • Farm produce reaches the markets fresh and fetches good prices because . . .
    • Water can be supplied easily to crops because . . .
    • Because farmers are making good profits . . .

▲ **C** *Favourable conditions for farming on the Plain of Lombardy*

The River Po and its tributaries drain the Plain of Lombardy. For centuries it has flooded and deposited fertile mud and silt over the land. Flooding is now less frequent but is still a danger in such a low-lying area. The level **relief**, however, does have advantages. Machinery is more economical to use and irrigation canals are easy to construct. In the north of Italy the winters are cold. The average January temperatures are 0–3°C, but summers are hot at 20°–35°C. The annual rainfall is 800mm which is a moderate amount. Unlike in the south, the rain falls all the year round.

▲ **D** *About the Plain of Lombardy*

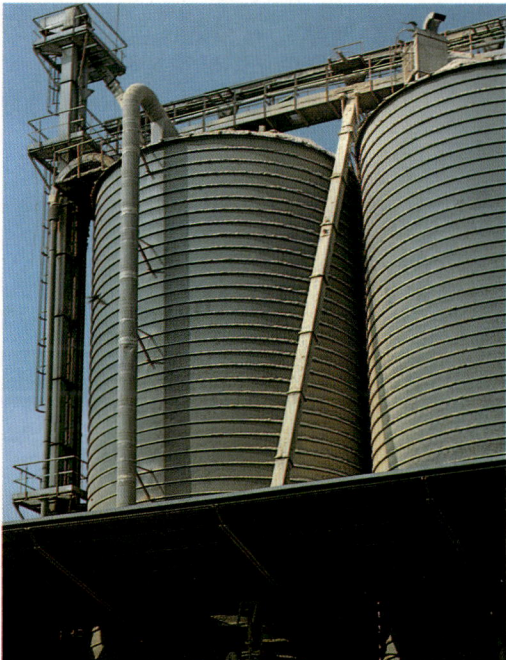

E *Efficient farming 1: a rice silo for proper storage*

F *Efficient farming 2: stall feeding in winter*

Glossary

Arête steep ridge between two **tarns**

Business parks planned areas of office and warehouse activities

Conurbation very large **urban** area formed when separate towns and cities join to become one built-up area

Derelict land land fallen into disuse

Employment structure balance of different types of job

European Community (EC) organization with 12 European member countries whose aim is to work together for greater economic, social and political cooperation and development

EC policies regulations about how the **EC** aims are carried out

Geographic region large area in which natural features have produced a distinct landscape

Growth pole planned concentrations of industry in southern Italy

Heavy industries industrial plants producing bulky goods on a large scale

Industrial estates planned areas of factories and warehouses

Industrial parks planned areas of factories and warehouses

Infrastructure basic power and water services and communications of an area

Invested (money) money provided for development

Locational factors reasons why economic activities are set up in certain places

Manufacturing industries businesses making goods

Mental images people's ideas about places

Migrated moved home to a different part of the country, or abroad

National Parks large areas which have been identified as having landscapes that are particularly attractive, usually in upland areas

Network system of linked routes

Outwash material sand, rocks and mud washed out and sorted by running water

Population density measure of how crowded or empty of population an area is

Quality of life description of the level of human welfare and well-being

Relief shape of the land

Reservoir lake used to store water for drinking and other commercial purposes

Restore change and improve land to make it useful

Ria long, narrow bay or inlet on a sea coast, caused by a rise in the sea level

Ribbon lake long valley bottom lake, cut by a glacier

Rural countryside area

Satellite images pictures of the earth's surface taken from space

Science parks planned estates of hi-tech industries

Screes broken fragments of rock which fall down a slope

Service jobs employment in which a job is done in e.g. shops, offices and public or private services

Soil erosion wearing away of the soil

Tarn hollow near a mountain top, cut by a glacier, and containing a lake

Trading buying and selling of goods

Urban area of towns and cities